Supporting and Supervising your Teaching Assistant

145-
147-(19)

Also available from Continuum:

How to be a Successful Teaching Assistant, J. Morgan

Teaching Assistant's Guide to Managing Behaviour, J. Morgan

Supporting and Supervising your Teaching Assistant

JILL MORGAN AND
BETTY Y. ASHBAKER

continuum

Continuum International Publishing Group

The Tower Building
11 York Road
London, SE1 7NX

80 Maiden Lane, Suite 704
New York,
NY 10038

www.continuumbooks.com

British Library Cataloguing-in-Publication Data
A catalogue record for this book is available from the British Library.

ISBN: 9781847063847 (paperback)

Library of Congress Cataloging-in-Publication Data
A catalog record of this book is available from the Library of Congress

Typeset by BookEns Ltd, Royston, Hertfordshire
Printed and bound in Great Britain by Antony Rowe, Chippenham, Wiltshire

Contents

Introduction

The profile of Teaching Assistants in the UK has been greatly raised in recent years due to:

◆ the National Agreement, 'Raising Standards and Tackling Workload', or Workforce Remodelling initiative (of 2003), which not only took steps to reduce unnecessary paperwork and bureaucracy for teachers, but also reviewed support staff roles and introduced the new roles of Higher Level Teaching Assistants (HLTAs) and cover supervisors
◆ the introduction of the Foundation Phase in Wales, and the Foundation Stage in England
◆ the Classroom Assistant Initiative in Scotland, launched as a pilot programme in 1998 and rolled out over the following three years.

These documents have all had a significant impact on how Teaching Assistants (TAs) are seen within the education system, and on the various ways in which they are deployed. They have also served to acknowledge the critical role TAs now play in supporting teaching and learning.

Government figures show that the number of support staff working in schools in England almost doubled in the decade from 1995 to 2005, with an estimated full-time equivalent figure of almost 300,000. TAs form one of the fastest growing groups of support staff, with figures showing an increase from 61,300 to 148,500 in England for that period. To put these increases into perspective, from 1998 to 2005 the number of teachers only increased by ten per cent – from 399,000 to 440,000. In Scotland the number of Classroom Assistants has trebled since they were introduced in 1998, and they now play an integral role in supporting teachers across most primary and secondary schools. Schools in Northern Ireland employ at least 15,000 Classroom Assistants, and in Wales at least 8,000.

A 2007 Estyn report stated: 'The significant increase in support staff numbers means that senior teachers find it time-consuming to organize and deploy these staff.' This is a very real concern, and presumably underlies your motivation for reading this book. The Estyn report seeks to reassure us that 'there is evidence that TAs who are suitably qualified and supervised will make a difference to pupil achievement'. And therein, we believe, lies the value of this book. It has been written for teachers. Not only teachers who are currently assigned as supervisors or mentors to TAs, but for all teachers. With the rising numbers of TAs in UK classrooms in recent years (a trend that is unlikely to diminish for some time to come), if you are one of the few teachers who is not responsible for a TA in any way, it is likely that you soon will be, and this book should provide you with some of the preparation you will need. In addition, those teachers who aspire to headships or deputy headships will be better equipped to lead schools with an understanding of the issues surrounding the supervision of TAs.

One of the assumptions we are making in this book is that TAs are – in practical terms – members of the teaching staff. Gone are the days when they were referred to as *non-teaching staff* because their roles were essentially ancillary. Very few TAs now have completely non-teaching roles. Indeed, a good many of them have responsibility for supervising other TAs in their work as part of the teaching team. We acknowledge that there are many differences between the role of a qualified teacher and that of a TA – not least that of legal status, where the teacher has overall responsibility for all that happens in the classroom. However, there are now so many similarities between the work teachers and TAs do that for the purposes of our discussions throughout this book, when we refer to those who teach, we will be including TAs, and we will refer to their work as teaching. Even if they are not responsible for the whole cycle of planning, teaching and assessment, their roles within that cycle are such that we must consider them as teaching members of staff.

In 2007 the Department for Children, Schools and Families (DCSF) published a research report entitled 'Deployment and impact of support staff in schools'. It reported the findings from the second national survey of schools, conducted in the 2005/2006 school year, investigating the characteristics, use and impact of support staff in schools in England and Wales. (You can find details in the Appendix on how to access the full report online.) It investigated the roles of all support staff, including administrative and site-management staff. Some of the interesting findings from the research for our purposes include:

◆ about 90 per cent of TAs had some form of job description, and about two-thirds had received an appraisal in the past year

◆ two-thirds of TAs were supervised by a teacher, but about one in ten stated that they received no supervision at all (this was more prevalent at secondary level than primary)

◆ it is becoming increasingly common for schools to require specific qualifications and previous experience of TAs as a condition of employment

◆ only a third of the teachers who were line managers of support staff had received training or development to help them with this role

◆ most teachers do not have allocated planning or feedback time with the support staff they work with in the classroom; special schools are most likely to allocate (and pay for) time for teachers to plan with TAs, secondary schools least likely

◆ three-quarters of the training and development provided by teachers for support staff was informal support on the job

◆ approximately half of TAs participating in the research said that they were satisfied with their job; about three-quarters stated that they felt the school appreciated their work.

These are all aspects of a supervisor's role, and this is the context within which you work – one that includes a growing sector of the workforce who experience very varied versions and degrees of supervision for the work they perform.

The School Workforce Development Board suggests that TAs provide support in a variety of ways:

◆ **Support for learning** – enabling teaching expertise to be matched more closely to learning needs, as teachers are freed up to teach rather than completing clerical or administrative tasks. The Office for Standards in Education (Ofsted) found that 'delegation of clerical and administrative tasks enabled teachers to focus to a greater extent on improving the quality of teaching and learning'.

◆ **Inclusion and achievement** – support staff play a key role in encouraging pupil participation and learning, promoting positive behaviour and improving attendance, and impacting positively on the inclusion of pupils with special educational needs (SEN) in mainstream classrooms.

◆ **Building relationships** – support staff are often the mediators between different groups in the school because of their familiarity with pupils' background and culture, and the fact that they are often members of the local community and predominant culture.

◆ **Offering a broader curriculum** – as schools recruit support staff with a wider range of skills and expertise, and school support staff frequently manage clubs and after-school activities, they are able to expand and enrich the curriculum.

◆ **Delivering extended services** – early research suggests support staff are involved in delivering a wide range of activities in schools offering extended services, for example: mentoring; 'wraparound' childcare; individualized support; recreation/sporting activities; pastoral care; healthy schools initiatives; specialist teaching (e.g. family literacy, adult computer classes); out-of-hours study support; and administration and coordination requirements of all activities.

All of these serve to underscore the essential work TAs perform in our schools, and which you supervise if you work with a TA. This book is divided into chapters that address what we see as critical elements or components of the supervisory process. This is a brief overview of what you can expect to find in each chapter.

In Chapter 1 (Supervising the Classroom Team) we look at who you are responsible for. We consider the question, what is supervision? What do we mean by the term? Is it synonymous with *management* or *mentoring*? Or is it something quite different? The remaining chapters look at how you can effectively supervise your TA(s) – the strategies you can use and the procedures you can put in place to ensure a successful partnership with your TA – so first we must be sure that we agree on basic concepts. In this regard we also therefore look at the government and legal guidelines for supervision, and consider how they apply to your situation.

Chapter 2 (Delegating Responsibilities). There are a number of justifications for delegating responsibilities to a TA, and in this chapter we look at what you can delegate within the law and within reason, as well as according to your own preferences and the guidelines set by the school and Local Education Authority (LEA). We look at the need for clear job descriptions for your TA based on her skills, training and experience, as well as on the needs of the children she supports. This is all within the context of LEA constraints and requirements for the local area where you work.

Chapter 3 (Accountability) looks at how you can monitor the quality of your TA's work. This is an uncomfortable topic for many teachers. We spend most of our days monitoring pupil performance and adjusting our teaching according to their needs, but we baulk at the idea of monitoring the work of other adults. Perhaps we feel it goes against the culture we grew up in, that it denotes disrespect or discourtesy, even that it violates the other person's rights. Nevertheless, it makes both legal and instructional sense, and we take time to explore this as well as providing a framework for how you and your TA can work together on this aspect of your collaborative relationship. In this chapter we also look at different methods of observation and monitoring, and how you can set priorities for improvement. This is set within the context of different standards that have been developed for TAs' work, particularly the National Occupational Standards for Supporting Teaching and Learning, and the standards for HLTA status.

This leads us on to Chapter 4 (Providing Continuing Professional Development) where we first discuss some of the ways in which you can provide professional development opportunities for your TA. We look at the importance of recognizing that your TA – as an adult learner – will have many similarities with your pupils. However there are also some significant differences worth bearing in mind. To this end, we take a brief look at Social Constructivism as a set of learning theories, focusing on the work of Jean Piaget, Lev Vygotsky and Jerome Bruner. We then look at the professional resources you can make available to your TA to supplement the direct training you offer her.

Chapter 5 (Reflective Practice). In this chapter, we first have you consider your own situation as a reflective practitioner, before discussing how you can help your TA become a reflective practitioner as she works alongside you. But the discussion goes deeper than the levels generally accepted as constituting reflective practice, as we discuss the need for *critical reflection* – a much deeper level, where we learn to question the assumptions or meaning perspectives underlying our practice, not just the practice itself. And in keeping with the recommendations of Jack Mezirow, acknowledged expert in reflective practice, we discuss the importance of engaging in reflective discourse with your TA.

Chapter 6 (Collaboration) is where we consider the work you do in conjunction with your TA, and the work your TA may engage in with other adults (particularly other TAs). We look at collaboration from a variety of perspectives, including a situated learning or apprenticeship approach. Then we look at some of Meredith Belbin's research on effective teamwork, as well as Peter Senge's recommendations for learning organizations.

In Chapter 7 (Logistics) we look at some of the practicalities of supervision – hopefully dealing with all those nagging doubts you may have about how this can work. And if the thoughts run along the lines of, 'but where do I find the time?' or, 'the Head says there are no resources for TAs!' you are certainly not alone. Teachers are generally very practical creatures, already obliged to use great creativity to cover the required curriculum in the given time (rather like trying to fit a quart into a pint pot) so as a teacher you can no doubt immediately see the difficulties you will face in trying to find time and resources for supervising your TA. Fortunately, teachers are generally very resourceful, and this chapter should help you address some of those potential obstacles. We also look at how you can advocate for your TA – with the Headteacher and school management team – for outside professional development opportunities, and for her status on the staff, as well as assisting her in evidencing her competence through the development of a portfolio.

In the Appendix we have listed details of the large number of resources referred to in the chapters, as well as suggestions for where you can find additional materials for training and supporting your TA. We have also included a comprehensive list of references to the professional literature relevant to this topic.

As you read through this book, you will find a 'Reflect and apply' feature at regular intervals. This is designed to help you focus on both the theory and the practicalities of being a supervisor – and to try to translate the one into the other. Research suggests that problem-centred instruction of this type can be a valuable aid to learning, and certainly the process of reflecting on what you have read should increase the likelihood of your remembering it, and putting it into practice.

And lastly, just a note or two about some of the conventions we have used in the book.

1. We refer to *your TA* but we recognize that you may be responsible for more than one – in the case of a SENCO no doubt several, and in a secondary school the number of TAs will certainly be in double figures. So the advice that we give here, although it appears to be for teachers supervising a single TA, is being presented for all teachers who supervise TAs, including those of you who work with TAs in the plural.

2. We use the pronoun *she* to refer to TAs. This is because all of the documentation on TAs shows that most (and that is up to 98 per cent) of TAs are female. Rather than use the rather awkward *he/she* we address what are evidently the majority, hoping that the minority will not be offended.

You may feel that you are not a natural leader – or even feel that it is necessary to lead your classroom or instructional team in a particularly assertive way. Or perhaps you feel that you already take your leadership responsibilities seriously, and take deliberate steps to build your classroom team and take them forward. Whichever is the case, we believe that this book can provide you with practical ways in which you can build your leadership skills as you become more aware of the many facets of your role as a supervisor of TAs. It can also help you develop a plan, or build a framework for systematically supervising your TA. We certainly believe that the book will provide you with food for thought, as we discuss the different aspects of your role from a variety of perspectives.

1 | Supervising the Classroom Team

If you work with a TA, whether you have considered yourself a supervisor or not, you have – by default – been the supervisor of a TA, and you will have gone about it in particular ways. So before we discuss the purposes and requirements for supervision, let's take some time to think about what you have been doing and why you have been doing it. In the same way that you have a particular and personal approach to your teaching and the way you manage your classroom, you will also have adopted a particular approach to working with your TA.

Reflect and apply

First take a moment to consider your assumptions about the work of a TA in your classroom and what your relative positions are, as teacher and TA working together. Ask yourself these questions:

- Do I see myself as 'in charge' and the TA as my subordinate, or are we partners in the teaching process?
- How much authority do I think my TA should have – complete freedom to use her own judgement, or does she always have to refer decisions to me?
- Do I see my TA as a person with a wide range of skills and assets, or as someone who can only be assigned a limited range of tasks because of a lack of qualifications or knowledge?

These are questions you should continue to ask yourself as you work with your TA, because they will have a direct influence on the way you work together. Take a moment to consider these questions and make a note of your responses.

→ continued

Styles of supervision

Below you will find brief descriptions of three different approaches or styles of supervision. Read each one through and then take some time to reflect on whether your current approach is similar to or different from each of them.

This is the situation. You have been assigned a TA. Let's call her T. She was assigned to your class because you have a number of children experiencing some difficulties. None of them has been identified as having special educational needs or additional learning difficulties, but the school where you work is in a deprived area and the children are definitely disadvantaged by it, so it was felt that an extra pair of adult hands in the classroom would be helpful.

Style 1: Hands-off/laissez-faire

Because T. is a capable adult – she's in her early 30s and has a young child of her own – you feel that you can trust her to see what needs to be done and make herself useful without too much guidance. Indeed since she's been working with you, you've noticed the difference that an extra pair of hands can make. When the class comes in every morning, she helps to take in homework and attends to various aspects of organization, and when it's time to clear up at the end of lessons or the end of the day she's there to help organize and keep pupils from getting distracted. She doesn't wait to be told what to do, but always makes herself useful – sitting and working with individual pupils or groups when you set them work to do; organizing and tidying up when you're teaching the whole class; or sitting listening to the instructions you give the class so that she knows what's expected. She knows that if she has any concerns she can come to you with them, and you do check with her on a regular basis that everything's OK. She always says she's fine and that she'll let you know if she needs anything. And she will occasionally ask a question about what a particular pupil is supposed to be doing or whether pupils should be working independently. Sensible questions from a very sensible woman. So you adopt a hands-off/ laissez-faire approach and see no need to be heavy-handed, checking up on her all the time.

Style 2: Equal partners

T. is a capable adult, so you are confident that you can work well together. You can see that as a young mother she brings valuable experience of child development and behaviour to the classroom team, and feel that she can contribute useful insights into how you can manage the classroom together. She doesn't have much by way of formal qualifications (she worked in a business office before becoming a TA), but she has a good deal of common sense and very good organizational skills – which is a real asset as it's not your strongest area. She is also obviously willing to learn, so you make a point of telling her why you do things in a particular way, and giving her some direction in the tasks you'd like her to take on and how she could best do them. She takes this well and will sometimes make suggestions as to how you could do things differently. Nothing inappropriate – more like suggestions and phrased in terms of, 'Do you think we could try …?' She feels like an ally in the classroom. On wet days or when the class seems to be playing up, you value her support, and the pair of you often sit together over a coffee during break-time and chat about what's happened during the day so far. You don't give her instructions for every minute of the day – you tell her what's planned and give her some level of choice in how she wants to participate with each of the learning activities. She sometimes asks if she can get on with some organizational task or make some resources while you're working with the whole class, but she will always stop what she's doing if you ask her to help a particular child or work with a group to keep them focused. It really does feel like a partnership. You know you have overall responsibility for the classroom, but T. pulls her weight and you know you couldn't manage without her.

Style 3: Hands-on

T. is a capable and sensible woman, so you know that she will not object to being shown how she should go about her work. In fact, you are sure that she will appreciate knowing exactly what's expected of her, because then she can be confident that she won't step on any toes and get into areas of responsibility that are beyond her remit and employment as a TA. To this end, you have drawn up a timetable for T.'s work, so for each part of the day she knows exactly who she should be working with. As you keep to a strict timetable, this is easily done and the subject areas and class groupings are decided in advance. You've prepared a file for T. where you keep notes on procedures and events (set by the school and for your class – things like fire-drills and school photographer's visits), and where you've asked her to keep notes on the work she does with pupils. As you recognize that she can't be expected to do this in her own time, you have asked her to do it at the end of each day or lesson while you are tying up ends with the class, conducting a plenary session or reading the current class story book. T. knows that her work is very much appreciated, but you have made it clear to her that her role is one of support and that she should refer instructional and behaviour management decisions to you. You have, however, discussed your behaviour management preferences with her so that she can be consistent in applying sanctions and using the merit system for appropriate behaviour. Teaching is a science and you want to be sure that your pupils have the best possible chance of success, so you use a hands-on approach with T. to ensure that she is an able and reliable deputy in the areas of responsibility assigned to her.

Reflect and apply

Which of these styles aligns most closely with your preferred style of supervision? Perhaps yours is a mix of two or more. You may wish to go through each of the styles and highlight the elements you feel are especially useful in each. You may also wish to underline or highlight aspects of each of those styles that cause you some concern or level of discomfort.

We might ask ourselves which of these styles is the correct one. But that question suggests that the others would be wrong. Each of them has advantages and disadvantages:

◆ The *hands-off/laissez-faire* style is one where the teacher just waits to see what will happen. If it isn't too much of a problem, she will ignore it or let it go until something must be done. It is a style that would work to a certain extent with a TA who is motivated and who understands the limits of her role, but otherwise it could be considered rather a risky way to supervise another adult in the classroom.

◆ The *equal partner* style is one where the teacher seems to forget she is the one who is ultimately responsible for the classroom. TAs do not have the training needed to make decisions that will affect student teaching and learning. But it is also a style that recognizes that the TA brings valuable assets to the team, and that teacher and TA can work together as partners.

◆ The *hands-on* style is proactive and prepares the way for the teacher and TA to work together. It provides information upfront rather than waiting for the TA to ask for it. However, even this style should be used with caution and sensitivity, as it can seem rather prescriptive and may suggest to the TA that she is incapable of making decisions for herself.

We are not suggesting that any one style is intrinsically right or wrong, but as you read through this book and complete the 'Reflect and apply' activities you will have opportunities to think about the different aspects of supervision referred to in these scenarios and consider which are the most effective ways for you to work with your TA.

Who are you responsible for?

In your work as a teacher you may come across TAs in a variety of ways. These might include:

◆ a TA assigned to your classroom full- or part-time
◆ a TA who comes into your classroom accompanying a child with a statement of special educational needs or Individual Education Plan (IEP), she may provide physical support by scribing for the child or social support by helping the child participate as part of the class

◆ a TA assigned to support a child with behavioural issues and who accompanies that child throughout the school day to keep him or her on task and focused on the work.

But which of these TAs would you consider to be your responsibility? Would you be considered the supervisor in all of these situations? Hopefully, your Headteacher will make it clear to you if you have supervisory responsibilities for a TA (or more than one), and what that supervision entails. But whenever you have contact with a TA, you should ask yourself what level of supervisory responsibility you have for her, and what the nature of that supervision should be. A situation that is becoming far more common now, is the TA who moves around between classes in secondary school to support a particular child. What responsibility does the subject teacher have for that TA and for supervising her? In many secondary schools, TAs are now assigned to subject teams, with each team lead by a head of department or other teaching member of staff. So can the subject teacher be excused from responsibility for supervising a TA in that situation? This raises the question of what we really mean by supervision — what is it for, and what does it look like in the classroom?

What is supervision?

Definitions

The term *supervision* may not come naturally to you in relation to working with a TA. There may be other terms that seem more appropriate, such as *management*. And yet you may be part of a management team at your school, but not necessarily consider yourself a manager — certainly not a manager of people. Teachers are accustomed to managing behaviour and learning, but typically this is children's behaviour and learning, not that of adults. Perhaps you have been assigned to be a *mentor* to a student teacher or other individuals on school placement, and this may be a more comfortable term for you to use in relation to your TA. For the purposes of our discussions in this book we will use the words *supervise* and *supervision* but consider them as synonymous with mentoring and management in that they all include responsibility to guide, monitor and support the work of another person — generally (but not invariably) one who is less well qualified or experienced.

Purposes of supervision

We will discuss the legal requirements for supervision later in the chapter. But first we may ask ourselves: Why supervision? What is its purpose? The remainder of the book will look at *how* to best supervise your TA, so we should first determine why teachers need to provide supervision in the first place (apart from the legal requirement to do so). Much of the literature and research relating to supervision of TAs comes from the United States. Thomas Sergiovanni and Robert Starratt, for example, in their 1993 book *Supervision: A Redefinition,* have said that supervision (which they call 'clinical' or in-class supervision), if used correctly, can create powerful results in improving instruction. They define it as 'face-to-face contact with teachers with the intent of improving instruction and increasing professional growth'. They list seven phases of clinical supervision in the classroom:

1. establishment of the [supervisor and supervisee] relationship
2. intensive planning of lessons and units [with the TA]
3. planning of a classroom observation strategy by teacher and TA
4. careful analysis of the teaching/learning process
5. planning a conference strategy
6. conference
7. resumption of planning

They identified the mental and physical closeness between the supervisor and supervisee as one of the most important principles of clinical supervision: that 'close and frequent proximity' is necessary to using a clinical supervision model.

Two decades prior to this statement, Richard Weller in his 1971 book *Verbal Communication in Instructional Supervision* had defined the purpose of clinical supervision as a series of systematic cycles of:

1. planning
2. observation
3. intensive intellectual analysis of teaching performance in the interest of rational modification

This statement was referring to supervision of teachers or student teachers rather than TAs. But from about the mid-1980s, a number of scholars working with TAs began to develop lists of supervisory activities that closely followed these models. (You will find details of the work of these scholars in the reference list in the Appendix.) We give an example in the box of one of the lists of supervisory activities, in this case by two American researchers, Stan Vasa and Alan Steckelberg.

Stan Vasa and Alan Steckelberg identified specific issues that supervising teachers face. These included:

◆ making daily assignments and scheduling activities
◆ designing instruction for another adult to carry out
◆ monitoring student progress and making instructional decisions when not present
◆ providing corrective feedback to paraprofessionals (TAs)
◆ developing and documenting on-the-job training
◆ evaluating paraprofessional/TA performance
◆ dealing with problems and differences.

From: Vasa, S. and Steckelberg, A.L. (1997)

If you look at the common theme between these authors, you will see that they agree that supervision is intended to improve instruction. In addition, both Weller's cycle and Sergiovanni and Starratt's recommendations sound a lot like action research as they recommend repetition of the steps and activities. This suggests more than just casual lip-service. It is *intensive* analysis of teaching performance so that we can make changes to improve quality or effectiveness. If this begins to feel uncomfortable, with performance suggesting *performance evaluation* or *appraisal*, take comfort in the remainder of Weller's phrase: *in the interest of rational modification*. We are not expected to make enormous changes overnight, or perform unreasonable feats of professional development. The important thing is to seek — as all good teachers do with their pupils — to make the small, incremental changes that constitute learning, and that eventually produce an expert — a child who is a confident reader, a child who understands spelling rules, a child who has grasped mathematical concepts and can work with them, a teacher who is perfecting his or her craft, or a TA who understands the teaching process and can therefore be an able assistant to the teacher and to the children they are jointly responsible for.

Reflect and apply

These are obviously very practical day-to-day activities or responsibilities that a teacher might undertake in supervising a TA. We might say that they provide a skeleton or framework for a supervisor's work. As you read through the remainder of the book you will be able to flesh out the details of these responsibilities, but always bear in mind that the primary purpose is to improve teaching.

Meanwhile, take time to think about the things that you currently do to supervise your TA. Look at the list provided by Vasa and Steckelberg.

◆ Do you do any of those things for or with your TA?
◆ Are there any that you do not currently do, but could?
◆ Do you provide feedback to your TA, or develop on-the-job training for her?
◆ How do you do these things?
◆ Could you do more of them?

Government and legal guidelines

The 2003 National Agreement 'Raising Standards and Tackling Workload', which we have already referred to in the Introduction, specified work regulations for support staff and provided associated guidance to clarify the role of support staff and 'a proper system of direction and supervision for them'. The National Agreement relates to all support staff (including clerical and janitorial staff) in both England and Wales, and a great deal of attention has been paid to the ways in which teachers can now delegate responsibilities to TAs, particularly as cover supervisors for their Preparation Planning and Assessment (PPA) time. Less public attention has thus far been given to the requirement for a 'proper system of direction and supervision' and what that really means. But you should be aware that it is there in the regulations, even if it has not yet been well defined, and that what you provide may be the closest form of supervision your TA receives.

In 2005, as part of the Primary National Strategy, the DfES published 'The effective management of Teaching Assistants to improve standards in Literacy and Mathematics' with an accompanying DVD.

As this document states:

> Teaching assistants play a key role as schools implement the workforce reforms set out in the National Agreement for raising standards and tackling workload. Recent reports published by HMI, the Primary National Strategy, university researchers and others show that well-trained and well-managed teaching assistants can have an impact on inclusion, children's achievements and attitude, and teacher workload.

The booklet and DVD were developed primarily for senior management staff, but contain useful guidance for anyone who works with, and has responsibility for, TAs. Details of how to obtain these materials are in the Appendix under the DCFS website. In Scotland, TAs are referred to as Classroom Assistants, and are considered non-teaching staff. Their role is to support pupil learning and to support the teacher, particularly in freeing up the teacher to teach by taking on administrative and routine tasks. You will find an interesting report on the Classroom Assistant Initiative – implemented in Scotland beginning in 1998 – on the Scottish Council for Research in Education website (details in the Appendix), if you are interested in finding out more.

From the research

In their 2005 book *Teachers and Assistants Working Together*, Karen Vincett, Hilary Cremin and Gary Thomas refer to 'tensions' in the classroom that prevent, or at very least reduce the likelihood of, effective collaboration or teamwork between teachers and TAs. These tensions include:

- ◆ TAs' lack of training or knowledge of effective classroom practices
- ◆ TAs' concern about their own status
- ◆ a lack of time for teachers and TAs to meet for joint planning
- ◆ a lack of effective teamwork between teachers and TAs
- ◆ the teacher's lack of knowledge of how best to work with TAs
- ◆ a lack of research into the impact of TAs' work on pupil achievement
- ◆ teachers not knowing how to use TAs to promote inclusion
- ◆ TAs' concerns about a lack of clarity over their role.

To overcome these tensions, Karen Vincett and her colleagues offer three models for organizing teams in classrooms:

1. Room Management
2. Zoning
3. Reflective Teamwork.

Room Management arose out of the recognized difficulty all teachers experience in trying to attend to individual learning needs (generally by working with small groups) while simultaneously making sure that the rest of the class are gainfully employed. The Room Management model recommends that if two adults are working in the classroom, one should be designated the Learning Manager (and work intensively with a small group or an individual) and the other the Activity Manager (who supervises the work of the larger group or remainder of the class). This larger group may be divided into smaller groups, but the nature of the supervision is necessarily less intense, as the Activity Manager has to oversee the work of so many pupils. The teacher or the TA can take either role, and there are arguments for both sides – should the teacher, being the expert, work with the children who need the most intense supervision, or should the teacher take responsibility for the larger number of pupils so that the TA can work with a small group, which is usually easier to handle?

Zoning is a system of classroom management and teamwork that defines the adult roles largely by location. The classroom is divided into zones or learning areas, and each adult knows exactly which zones he or she is responsible for. The zones may be based on an already existing arrangement of work tables where children are normally sitting in groups, or they could be smaller units literally separated into physical zones by bookcases or other barriers. Zoning responsibilities can be changed at any time, as long as each adult recognizes the physical boundaries of his or her new responsibility.

Whereas the above models are based very much on the need for *role clarity*, with each adult working quite separately, *Reflective Teamwork* is designed to enhance levels of *planning, communication* and *review*. Using this model, teachers and TAs are encouraged to sit together daily for about 15 minutes to review previous teaching sessions. First the TA and then the teacher identifies two things that went well during a particular teaching session, as well as two things that could be improved upon. This reflection is then worked into planning for upcoming teaching sessions.

If you look back at the tensions listed by Vincett and colleagues, you will see that their Reflective Teamwork model aims to counteract many of the tensions listed:

- the **TA's lack of training/knowledge about classroom practice** can be counteracted by the teacher providing on-the-job training and insights into effective practice as she discusses the strengths and weaknesses of different teaching sessions
- the **TA's concern about status** can be counteracted by the teacher giving credence to the TA's views and showing that her opinion is valued
- dedicating just 15 minutes each day to team reflection helps to counteract the perceived **lack of time for teachers and TAs to meet and plan together**
- the structured 15 minutes of team reflection counteracts the **teacher's lack of knowledge of how best to work with TAs.**

Reflect and apply

Do any of these models sound like how you organize the division of labour with your TA? Have you tried to work in any of these ways? Has it been successful? And if not, what particular difficulties have you found? How have you been able to overcome or prevent those difficulties? Take a minute or two to jot down your thoughts in response to these questions.

_____

_____

_____

_____

_____

_____

Chapter summary

As a teacher who works with TAs, you are the leader of the classroom team. You may already have a system in place and an understanding with your TA(s) about how you like to work, or – at the other extreme – you may be in a position where TAs work in your classroom but not necessarily under your control. Whichever is true, you do have responsibility to ensure that you follow legal and ethical guidelines in using and supervising TAs. Government documentation states that TAs should be systematically supervised. While it may be the responsibility of a school's senior management team to ensure that proper systems are in place, the reality is that you are the person who works with the TA on a day-to-day basis, so you also need to be clear about what your responsibilities are, and for whom. We have discussed some of the possible ways in which TAs can be supervised in this chapter, and will go into more detail in the remaining chapters of the book. Schools heavily rely on TAs now – more than ever – and they can encourage teachers and TAs to plan and conference together, and carry out the activities recommended by those who have researched these issues. But as the teacher, you will need to take the lead to ensure that your classroom team functions most effectively to support children's learning.

2 | Delegating Responsibilities

A great deal has been written both in government documentation and in the academic literature about the roles of TAs, and you will find a variety of references on this topic in the Appendix. Articles and official documents have typically addressed such questions as:

◆ how TA roles have developed from being largely ancillary and clerical to being much more technical and firmly rooted in the teaching and learning processes
◆ what constitutes an appropriate role for a TA
◆ who should decide what roles TAs take on.

Of course, the answers to these sorts of questions will differ according to where you work — in terms of your LEA but also according to whether you come under the auspices of Westminster or the education departments of Scotland, Wales or Northern Ireland. They also depend on whether you work in an early years setting, special unit or facility for pupils with special needs, or indeed at secondary level. One thing remains common to all decisions about TA roles in this respect: the minute detail of what your TA does is decided in your classroom, between you and your TA.

We have framed this chapter as a series of questions that you may ask yourself about delegation of responsibilities to your TA. They are:

◆ What responsibilities were assigned to my TA as part of the employment process and how do they relate to my classroom?
◆ How carefully do I need to define my TA's responsibilities?
◆ What responsibilities can I reasonably and legally delegate to my TA?

What responsibilities were assigned to my TA as part of the employment process and how do they relate to my classroom?

There are no absolute requirements for prior education and training when it comes to employing TAs. However, although there are no official set entry requirements, schools and LEAs are increasingly looking to employ TAs with some level of experience and training, and those who are considering applying for positions are encouraged to acquire nationally recognized qualifications (a selection of which you will find in the box). Of course, an understanding of English and maths is important in order to support the development of basic literacy and numeracy skills in the classroom, and previous, relevant experience (nursery nurse, playgroup worker, youth worker) may help. Many TAs have begun their work in schools as parent volunteers, which has not only given them experience of classrooms, but has allowed the school to gain direct knowledge of how well they relate to children and work under the direction of the teacher. And many other TAs begin their school experience as part of a course designed to train them as teaching assistants.

Vocational qualifications suitable for TAs with little or no previous experience:

- CACHE Level 2 Certificate for Teaching Assistants

- NCFE Level 2 Certificate

- BTEC Level 2 Certificate

- ABC Level 2 Certificate

Those who have successfully completed Level 2 can work towards their Level 3 Certificate for TAs. NVQs/SVQs in Early Years Care and Education at Levels 2 and 3 for TAs are also available for those already working in the classroom.

In Scotland, newly recruited Classroom Assistants can pursue Professional Development Awards at colleges of further education on a part-time, day-release or evening basis. Some universities offer certificates/diplomas of higher education or foundation degrees specifically for TAs. Modern Apprenticeships have also now been developed for TAs. They provide a work-based route to recognized qualifications, and can lead onto higher-level qualifications, with slightly different arrangements for Apprenticeships in Scotland, Wales and Northern Ireland. There is of course no upper age limit for starting in this type of work, and many schools prefer people who have had experience of working with or raising their own children.

Thus when a TA is first employed by a school or LEA, expectations for their role will generally be based on a job description developed to advertise the post. However, this is likely to be quite generic, and will need to be developed to more closely match what she is expected to do in your classroom on a daily basis. That means the specific support she will be providing to specific pupils according to their individual needs. You can find a sample job description for a TA on the government's 'Teachernet' website. The elements it covers are outlined in the box.

Teaching assistant – Elements of a sample job description

Post: Teaching assistant
Responsible to: Headteacher
Job purpose: [optional]
Responsible for: [optional]

Duties

The job description describes anticipated duties in general terms, as the precise nature of the TA's responsibilities may change due to changing school circumstances, without affecting the essential nature of the job.

Teaching and learning

Duties in relation to supporting teaching and learning should be described here, including reference to the member of staff under whose direction the TA will work, and the types of pupils she may work with – those with IEPs, for example.

Administrative duties

Duties in relation to clerical and administrative work should be described here, including meetings the TA will be expected to attend.

Other duties and responsibilities

Other duties that the Headteacher might occasionally assign to the TA should be listed here.

Reflect and apply

Take a moment, then, to list the responsibilities assigned to your TA. (If you work with more than one, you probably need to do this for each one, as they are unlikely to have exactly the same responsibilities.) As you list the responsibilities, be quite specific about what those responsibilities entail.

_____

_____

_____

_____

_____

_____

As you look over what you have written you may have included items such as:

◆ listen to children read, or
◆ provide general support, or
◆ sit with Jack and keep him focused on his work.

These are all very open to interpretation. If you do not mind your TA interpreting your instructions liberally, then that is not a problem. But if you have particular ways in which you would like things done, then you will probably be disappointed unless you are very specific about what you ask your TA to do.

How carefully do I need to define my TA's responsibilities?

Many teachers have said to us over the years, 'Oh I just tell her to make herself useful – she's an adult, after all, so she can see what needs doing.' Have you ever given your TA this sort of guidance? Perhaps not, but let's take a moment to consider the implications – for you, your TA, and for the children you both support.

Let's make an analogy with your home. Telling a TA to 'make herself useful' is rather like telling someone to make themselves at home in your house. Now when you say that, you may really mean it. But have you ever had guests (or family members or friends) who have interpreted that invitation a touch too liberally? Who have literally taken liberties in your home? It is worth asking yourself, *'When I say "make yourself at home", what exactly do I mean?'* After all, your teenage children or housemates make themselves at home, and that may mean:

◆ walking into the house without knocking or ringing
◆ leaving their dirty laundry on the bathroom floor for you to pick up (and wash, of course)
◆ inviting large numbers of friends in while you are out, and ransacking the freezer to feed them all
◆ playing loud music or shutting themselves in their room to play computer games and not coming out for hours
◆ borrowing your car without asking.

This may be what family members do, and you may be OK with it. Or perhaps you resent it somewhat, but choose to put up with it. But is it what you would expect or want just anyone to do?

Let's go back to your classroom where you have essentially told your TA to 'make herself at home'. What do you really mean by that? Is it OK if she:

◆ tidies or clears the papers on your desk?
◆ rearranges classroom furniture without consulting you, or reorganizes cupboards and drawers so that everything is in a different place?
◆ makes use of your belongings, resources and equipment without asking?
◆ sets her own schedule, or changes what you've asked her to do because she prefers to do things differently, or feels they can be done more effectively in a different way?
◆ leaves papers or materials she's been using out on the work surfaces or children's tables?
◆ adjusts the curriculum for some students without your input?

These are all ways in which a TA could make herself useful and at home in the classroom, but which of these would you want her to do? Perhaps none of them; or perhaps you would be perfectly comfortable with any of them. Most of those responses are acceptable, but – as with your home and immediate family or housemates – you have to weigh up what you would really like, what you can live with if you have to, and what you really can *not* tolerate. Otherwise, you are looking at a recipe for chaos and conflict. You can avoid problems with this type of situation by being clear about the work you are delegating to your TA and what her responsibilities are, and by giving directions that are specific – which we will come back to a little later. In the box you will find another example of a job description – this time from one of the Scottish boards of education advertising for a Classroom Assistant. You will notice that this job description is much more specific than the previous example, giving much more detail of what will be required, including examples of activities that a Classroom Assistant may be required to carry out.

JOB DESCRIPTION – Classroom Assistant (Scotland)

POST TITLE: Classroom Assistant (Primary – Non-teaching)

JOB PURPOSE: Assist the class teacher in administrative, practical and organizational tasks; support the learning activities of pupils.

MAJOR TASKS. DUTIES TYPICALLY INCLUDE:

1. Contribute to the effective organization and use of resources.
   1.1 Organize and maintain materials and distributing resources.
   1.2 Maintain and catalogue collections of resources, e.g. libraries, collections of computer software, mathematics equipment.
   1.3 Prepare class materials by duplicating, setting out and clearing away equipment, making booklets.
   1.4 Make displays, e.g. mounting examples of children's work, pictures, interest tables under the supervision of teaching staff.
   1.5 Record educational television and radio programmes.
2. Contribute to the quality of care and welfare of pupils.
   2.1 Build good relationships in contacts with pupils.
   2.2 Encourage good standards of pupil behaviour.

→ *continued*

2.3 Supervise non-teaching areas, e.g. corridor, cloak-room, playground.

2.4 Supervise classes during 'wet playtimes'.

2.5 Escort pupils within and outside the premises, e.g. between classrooms, to home, on educational visits or swimming lessons.

2.6 Provide comfort and care for minor accidents, upsets or ailments, e.g. cuts and bruises (report to teaching staff if considered serious).

2.7 Help children who need support in putting on coats, shoes etc. while encouraging independence.

3. Support pupils in effectively accessing the curriculum.

3.1 Build a positive relationship with pupils and support the classroom/school ethos.

3.2 Develop good teamwork with the teacher and other staff.

3.3 Prepare the classroom for the day's work, e.g. setting up the art area or computer, setting out science apparatus.

3.4 Support pupils in paying attention, concentrating, staying on task.

3.5 Provide appropriate praise/encouragement to pupils during tasks.

3.6 Support children working together to encourage teamwork and cooperation.

3.7 Provide support to pupils in their classroom learning, e.g. use of computers and general class activities.

3.8 Help with tasks where there are physical difficulties, whilst encouraging independence and ensuring safety.

3.9 Help pupils to follow instructions, e.g. when changing activities.

3.10 Provide help to pupils in organizing their work and following classroom routines.

3.11 Provide information for teachers' records and progress reports.

3.12 Provide support to pupils in the dining hall.

4. Support the quality of learning and teaching in the classroom.

→ *continued*

4.1 Support children's play activities, e.g. by listening and talking with children, joining in play activities, supporting individual children.

4.2 Play games that practise skills, encourage sharing, turn-taking and cooperation.

4.3 Encourage children's oral language development through play, books, stories and personal interaction.

4.4 Support literacy development, e.g. by reading or telling stories, guiding pupils to information books, labelling drawings and models.

4.5 Support numeracy development, e.g. by counting/ matching games and rhymes, practising number bonds and 'tables', building with shapes, developing appropriate language.

4.6 Support practical activities in the classroom, planned as part of the teacher's programme, e.g. baking, gardening.

4.7 Supervise pupils as they undertake work set by the teacher.

4.8 Support record keeping by completing checklists of tasks with individual pupils where appropriate.

ESSENTIAL ATTRIBUTES

Minimum acceptable levels for safe and effective job performance

DESIRABLE ATTRIBUTES

◆ Experience of looking after young children and working with children with special needs, e.g. as a parent helper or lunchtime supervisor
◆ Qualification in Child Care and Education (or similar)
◆ Ability and commitment to undertake initial training and subsequent staff development as required
◆ Skills/abilities specific to post
◆ An understanding of the needs of parents with young children
◆ Ability to relate positively to young children and their parents
◆ A keen interest in child development

→ *continued*

INTERPERSONAL AND SOCIAL SKILLS

◆ Good interpersonal skills
◆ Enjoy working with children
◆ Flexible and adaptable approach
◆ Reliable and dependable
◆ Pleasant manner
◆ Ability to work as part of a team

We would add a note of caution here, because there are two sides to delegation of responsibilities. When you define your TA's role, you have to decide not only what you want her to do, but also what you do *not* want her to do. And if you do not tell her the things she is *not* supposed to do, she is not likely to know. She is no better a mind-reader than your children, partner or spouse. They may not know that a particular habit of their's bothers you – or that you love roses. Likewise, your TA needs to know when she is going beyond the bounds of what you consider reasonable behaviour in some of the things she habitually does in the classroom, just as much as she needs to know when you are pleased with the things she does. And not unlike your family members or room-mates, she may need to hear a message more than once before she remembers and does things the way you would like.

Reflect and apply

Now look back at the items you listed as your TA's responsibilities. For each, ask yourself, '*Have I been specific enough? Will my TA understand what this means?*' If your answer is *no* or *perhaps not*, then rewrite that statement in more specific terms.

As you review what you've written, adjust it as needed to make sure the statement will be understood by *all* TAs in your classroom.

_____

_____

_____

What responsibilities can I reasonably and legally delegate to my TA?

There are a number of headings under which teachers can delegate responsibilities to TAs. First there are the government guidelines that describe what can legally be delegated. Then there are your personal preferences as a teacher. In addition there is common sense – within reason, there are many tasks that can be shared with or delegated to your TA.

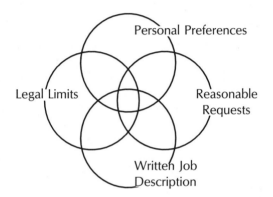

Figure 2.1. Delegation of responsibilities to TAs

Delegating responsibilities – Within the law

The National Agreement 'Raising Standards and Tackling Workload' acknowledged the pressure on schools to raise standards by tackling unacceptable levels of workload for teachers. It introduced a series of significant changes to teachers' conditions of service, to be introduced in three annual phases in England and Wales from September 2003. This type of agreement was not required for schools in Scotland, as the whole of the TA's role there is considered to be one of support to free up the teacher for teaching; hence their title of Classroom (rather than Teaching) Assistants. A fundamental element of the agreement is the recognition that a teacher is not always the most appropriate member of school staff to perform a particular duty. Teachers have the key role in relation to pupils' learning, but new support staff roles were created by the remodelling process:

◆ cover supervisors
◆ HLTAs
◆ bursars/school business managers
◆ pastoral managers
◆ invigilation staff.

Historically, many of a teacher's duties have had little or nothing to do with their core area of expertise: teaching and learning. Thus in many ways it makes sense to free up teachers to teach. The National Agreement also recognized that planning and preparation of lessons and pupil assessment are key elements of successful teaching, so it provided teachers with a guaranteed allocation of time for these activities during the school day (PPA time – typically one half day per week). A 2008 report of research commissioned by the Welsh Assembly, entitled 'School support staff in Wales' investigated the deployment of support staff in Welsh schools. Some interesting points were made in relation to the present discussion:

◆ The research previously published (in 2004) on Classroom Assistants in Scotland reported that their introduction had been welcomed by schools, relieving teachers of many mundane tasks and contributing to better learning conditions for pupils.
◆ The importance of support staff to the success of schools in Wales was widely recognized by teaching staff.
◆ Although it is difficult to quantify, the impact of TAs' work 'can be seen in improved academic results as their support improves pupils' basic skills and teachers are released by contractual changes arising from the workforce agreement from more mundane tasks to focus on raising pupil performance'.
◆ The impact of support staff could be enhanced through widening the roles they undertake, provided they were given appropriate training.
◆ Support staff generally stated that they enjoy their work, especially the contact with children. However they bring considerable goodwill to their roles, and many expressed a feeling of 'slight injustice' because many of the tasks they carry out would be considered a teacher's role, but for which they receive a fraction of a teacher's salary.

Any teacher will tell you that there is more to be done in a classroom than there is time for. The idea of delegating activities that are important to the classroom infrastructure, but not vital to pupil instruction and learning, is one that all teachers can support. The challenge, then, is to identify the activities and responsibilities that can be given over to someone else. This was made easier by the National Agreement specifying 25 tasks that were considered to be non-teaching tasks (24 in 2003, with the last one added for implementation in 2005) and that therefore could be delegated to TAs. You will find these 25 tasks listed in the box.

25 non-teaching tasks that should be transferred from teachers to support staff under the National Agreement.

◆ collecting money
◆ chasing absences: teachers can inform the relevant member of staff when students are absent
◆ bulk photocopying
◆ copy typing
◆ producing standard letters: teachers may contribute as appropriate in formulating the content of these letters
◆ producing class lists: teachers may be involved as appropriate in allocating students to a particular class
◆ record keeping and filing: teachers may contribute to the content of records
◆ classroom display: teachers determine what material is displayed in and around their classroom
◆ analysing attendance figures: teachers make use of the outcome of analysis
◆ processing exam results: teachers use the analysis of results
◆ collating pupil reports
◆ administering work experience: teachers may support pupils on work experience, through advice and visits
◆ administering examinations: teachers have responsibility for identifying appropriate examinations for their pupils
◆ administering teacher cover
◆ ICT troubleshooting and minor repairs
◆ commissioning new ICT equipment

→ *continued*

- ◆ ordering supplies and equipment: teachers may identify needs
- ◆ stocktaking
- ◆ cataloguing, preparing, issuing or maintaining equipment and materials
- ◆ minuting meetings: teachers may communicate action points from meetings
- ◆ coordinating and submitting bids: teachers make a professional input into the content of bids
- ◆ seeking and giving personnel advice
- ◆ managing pupil data: teachers make use of the analysis of data
- ◆ inputting pupil data: teachers make the initial entry of pupil data into school management systems
- ◆ invigilating examinations

The law then allows for quite considerable delegation of tasks to TAs – not only in terms of the 25 clerical/housekeeping tasks, but also in terms of the new roles introduced by the National Agreement.

Delegating responsibilities – Within reason

If we consider what you can *reasonably* delegate to your TA, logic suggests that you must consider two things:

- ◆ the purposes of the school and curriculum, the essence of which is individual pupil needs
- ◆ the skills and abilities your TA brings to her work.

You need to identify the things you currently do that you can delegate, but consider them in terms of your TA's experience and qualifications. Don't downplay the former in favour of the latter until you have determined what she really knows about effective classroom practices. Consider both instructional and behavioral practices. It really is a two-way street, isn't it? You must look at the expertise of the TA as well as the things that must be done to meet the needs of pupils.

Reflect and apply

List what you perceive or know to be your TA's talents, skills, and experience here. If you have more than one TA, add another sheet and write about each one separately.

_____

_____

_____

Without showing your TA what you have written, give her a sheet of paper and ask her to list her talents, skills, and experiences. Afterwards, the two of you can read what each has written and discuss your observations. This offers a rich opportunity to tell your TA about the many ways in which you value her contribution to the classroom, and recognize her talents and expertise.

You may wish to think about this in terms of 'what I know about my TA' and 'how this might contribute to her work'. If you list what you know of your TA's attributes, skills and experience down one side of a page, you can then make a note of how these could contribute to her work on the opposite side of the page. In addition, a book by Rosemary Sage and Min Wilkie (_Supporting Learning in Primary Schools_ – details in the Appendix) has a chapter dedicated to 'Developing your own learning' from the TA's perspective and includes a skills audit. You will also find a 'Self-evaluation of current skills and qualities' in Stella Cottrell's _Study Skills Handbook_. Although this is not specifically written for TAs, it offers another format for identifying and recognizing skills and attributes in your TA.

As a teacher, you are familiar with the cycle of planning, teaching/ learning and assessment, with each assessment informing the next round of planning, teaching/learning and assessment. This is often referred to as Assessment for Learning, or a formative assessment cycle. As a reminder, this is in direct contrast to summative assessment procedures such as SATs and standardized tests, which give a snapshot of a child's abilities at a certain point in time but provide the information in a format that gives insufficient detail for you to use the information to help the child with specific aspects of learning. You will find an example of summative assessment in the box.

Summative assessment

Take the example of a weekly spelling test. The summative result of 3 out of 10 only tells you that the child is a weak speller (or that the level of difficulty was misjudged). It does not tell you what sort of help the child needs to improve. For that you would need to see the actual test, in order to pinpoint patterns of good and poor spelling so that you could remediate in ways that are meaningful to the child.

We make this point for two reasons:

1. Your TA is probably not familiar with the terminology and may never have had the reasoning behind different forms of testing explained to her. So there is a training issue here for your TA in terms of pedagogy and education jargon.
2. Perhaps more importantly for this discussion of delegating responsibilities for TAs, you need to decide where your TA will participate in the learning cycle – which elements of it she will most usefully be able to contribute to.

As you look at tasks that might be delegated, consider what the job entails and why that type of work is necessary. In a nursery or primary school, with children aged 3–11, a TA can help in a variety of ways:

- getting things ready for lessons
- reading and telling stories
- helping children with number work by using counting games or learning tables
- playing games and encouraging children to play together
- talking and listening to children
- displaying arts and craft work
- supervising dining and play areas
- escorting pupils between classes and on outings and sports events.

TAs support teachers in schools as they work with individual children, small groups or the whole class. The work often involves helping children with special educational needs or those for whom the first language is not English.

◆ comforting and caring for children who have a minor accident or are upset
◆ helping younger children with motor and coordination skills such as holding pencils correctly or tying shoelaces
◆ helping the teacher to maintain records
◆ liaising with other professionals, parents and carers.

Many of these items are providing direct support to children's learning, and are not simply clerical or organizational roles.

Most TAs in secondary schools work as special needs assistants. This might involve accompanying a pupil around the school, taking notes in lessons or carrying bags and books. Secondary schools usually have learning support departments where TAs work with individuals or small groups of pupils, often complementing work being done in class. These are also roles that relate directly to learning, complementing the teacher's efforts and responsibilities. Table 2.1 provides an example of how instructional tasks can be shared between teacher and TA, with joint activities cementing individual responsibilities.

Table 2.1. An example of differentiated instructional roles for teachers and TAs

Teacher role	TA role	Areas of communication
Instruction		
– Plan all instruction, including small group activities – Provide instruction in whole-class settings	– Work with small groups of pupils on specific tasks, including review or re-teaching of content – Work with one pupil at a time to provide intensive instruction or remediation on a concept or skill	– Teachers provide specific content and guidance about pupils, curriculum, and instructional materials – TAs note pupil progress and give feedback to teachers
– Develop lesson plans and instructional materials – Ensure alignment with standards, pupil needs, and IEPs	– Provide assistance in development of classroom activities, retrieval of materials and coordination of activities	– Joint review of lesson plan prior to class – Teachers provide guidance about specific instructional methods
– Develop and guide class-wide management plans for behaviour and classroom structures – Develop and monitor individual behaviour management plans	– Assist with implementation of classwide and individual behaviour management – Monitor corridors and other activities outside normal class	– Teachers provide guidance about specific behaviour management strategies – TAs note pupil progress and give feedback to teachers
– Plan differentiation for pupils with special needs – Develop modified materials	– Guided by teacher and IEP, use differentiated material and methods (large print, taking notes, reading material aloud)	– Teacher guides TA in the use of differentiated material and ensures that TA is aware of IEP goals – TA provides feedback about pupil progress and success of adaptations
– Determine, create and administer appropriate formal and informal tests	– Assist in the administration of tests	– Teacher provides guidance on the content and administration of tests
– Determine modifications needed for pupils with special needs; use assessment results to inform future planning	– Implement modifications – Collect anecdotal evidence of pupil achievement on a regular basis	– TA provides feedback on pupil progress – Joint conversations about anecdotal evidence and informal data

Adapted from the 'Iris Center' website (http://iris.peabody.vanderbilt.edu) All materials are freely available to the public.

Reflect and apply

This is a good point at which to consider how and where your TAs can contribute to the teaching and learning cycle. This in terms both of how she does already contribute, and how she might contribute – i.e. what you can add to her contribution. Consider each of the elements in the diagram (planning, teaching/learning, assessment) and what contributions your TA makes to each of them. Take a moment to make some notes about where she contributes to the process.

_____

_____

_____

_____

_____

_____

This will connect later with the chapter on providing continuing professional development (CPD), because as the teacher you will determine her training needs and therefore where she can fit in with your teaching responsibilities.

Delegating responsibilities – Within my own professional and personal preferences

There is nothing to say that you have to hand over certain responsibilities to your TA. Even the 25 tasks specified by the National Agreement are legally allowable if you wish to carry them out. It is quite reasonable to factor your personal preferences into the decision of what to delegate to your TA. However, it does also make sense to delegate according to your individual assets and preferences. There are personal traits, skills and talents that a TA brings to the job. Some of these personal qualities include:

◆ being able to build good relationships with children, teachers, parents and carers;
◆ supporting and encouraging learning;
◆ enjoying taking responsibility and being well organized;
◆ being able to work well under the supervision of a teacher;
◆ understanding the importance of confidentiality;
◆ being aware of child protection and safety procedures;
◆ being patient and kind, but firm when necessary;
◆ having good spoken and written communication skills;
◆ being numerate;
◆ having lots of energy;
◆ being able to work with computers.

And, of course, you will want to consider your TA's preferences and talents. Talk to her about her responsibilities and how comfortable she is with them. Ask her if there are other things she would be interested in doing. If you have a good working relationship, you may well have already discussed her assignments with her, but she may need to be invited to make suggestions about her role.

Chapter summary

In this chapter we have been discussing the various bases on which you decide which roles and responsibilities to assign to your TA. These include what is legally allowable and recommended by government and other authorities, your own personal working preferences, and what might be considered reasonable given your TA's skills and prior experience. We have also considered the importance of developing a job description for your TA, and we hope that you see that a precise job description can help prevent potential difficulties and tensions, as it will enable your TA to understand both the extent and limits of her role. A TA's job description should be specific to her because it is a combination of the needs of the pupils assigned to her and the skills and abilities she brings to that assignment. This is the type of job description that is needed to keep the classroom running more smoothly, and ensures that your TA is truly providing support where and how it is needed.

3 | Accountability

This chapter is about accountability – whom you answer to as a teacher supervising a TA – and the many forms that that accountability may take. But it is also about your TA's accountability – she is accountable to you for what she does, and there are a variety of ways in which she can demonstrate that accountability and provide you with feedback on the responsibilities you have assigned to her. When we talk about accountability, we must of necessity also talk about evaluation in some form, because it is difficult to quantify or even describe one's work without making some sort of judgement about it, and accountability requires a weighing up of a person's work and efforts to see whether it matches what has been requested or required. We use the term evaluation here. You may prefer a word such as *monitoring* or *assessment*. For the purpose of this discussion we will consider all of these to be synonymous, but implicit is the notion that each has the purpose of monitoring to determine quality of work. Your real preference may be to talk about 'keeping an eye' on your TA or 'checking with/on her' but these all effectively mean the same. Some are obviously more formal – and you may have personal preferences for one particular terminology over another – but whatever you call it, this is something that you do as a teacher – as part of your teaching.

As we look at monitoring the quality of your TA's work, we also must of necessity look at the standards for excellence established for TAs, as well as discussing how you might go about setting priorities for improvement.

So let's first think in general terms about monitoring or evaluation. It is an essential part of the teaching process, and you engage in it on a daily or even hourly basis with your pupils.

Reflect and apply

What does monitoring or evaluation look like when you do it for and with your pupils? You may wish to write down some of the things you do to monitor what is going on in your classroom, and make a note beside each one as to why you do this. What does it tell you? How does it help you to teach?

What you do   Why you do it and what it tells you

_____   _____

_____   _____

_____   _____

The research shows (and you will find references to this research in the bibliography at the end of the book) that more effective teachers monitor the work of their pupils more often than less effective teachers – they also act on what they discover. In a well run classroom, the teacher has set up systems and procedures to ensure that things run smoothly, and that pupils know what is expected of them. In primary school classrooms, there are rules posted on the wall to remind the pupils how to conduct themselves, and there are organizational helps such as labelled drawers and other containers. Classrooms in primary and secondary schools will have systems for how and when homework is handed in or where textbooks are stored. But the best teachers don't just make these arrangements and rest on their laurels: they constantly monitor what is going on to see if the systems and procedures are working, or if they need to be adjusted in some way to make them more effective and efficient. If they are redundant, they abolish them. Likewise with teaching methods and strategies, effective teachers plan how they are going to facilitate learning experiences for their pupils, and then they monitor how well those strategies seem to be working, and change them if they seem to be ineffective. When teachers use systematic monitoring to track their pupils' progress in reading, maths or spelling, they are better able to identify which pupils are in need of additional or different forms of instruction, they design stronger instructional programmes and their pupils achieve more. This forms a cycle of planning, teaching and assessment that should be constant in effective classrooms.

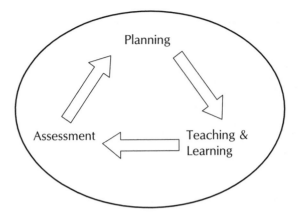

Figure 3.1. Planning – teaching/learning – assessment cycle

The main reasons you monitor what is going on in your classroom are likely to be:

- Checking what your pupils are doing and how well they are doing it (are they working on the task they should be working on, how engaged are they, and are they succeeding?).
- Assessing how well classroom procedures and organization are working. (Is the homework being put in the tray set aside for it, are the book-bags in the box once the children are all sitting down ready to start their day; do pupils enter the room and quickly settle or do they wander aimlessly around or chat until they are called to order? When they finish a piece of work, do they know what to do next?).
- Evaluating how effectively you are teaching, according to the responses of your pupils (are they looking bored, or avoiding eye-contact, or are they interested and eager to participate and answer your questions or make suggestions?).
- Checking to see whether your pupils are retaining information or understanding of concepts (can they answer questions you ask about yesterday's work, or explain a concept discussed last week?).

Just as you monitor the work of your pupils, you should monitor the work of your TAs. If you re-read the reasons for monitoring pupils you may decide that these reasons are very similar to why you monitor the work of your TAs.

Reasons for monitoring what is happening in the classroom

◆ checking what your pupils are doing and how well they are doing it;

◆ assessing how well classroom procedures and organization are working;

◆ evaluating how effectively you are teaching, according to the responses of your pupils.

Monitoring the quality of the TA's work

Your TA is your deputy – whether you are working together in the same physical teaching space or not. She is there to provide an extra pair of hands, eyes and ears. Because she is there you can spread the workload and potentially accomplish much more than you could if you were working alone. Because she stands in for you in this way, it is essential that you monitor the quality of her work. You want her to work the way you do – not necessarily using exactly the same methods and strategies, but certainly in the sense of using effective methods and strategies to facilitate pupils' learning. Without monitoring her work in some way, you will not be able to tell whether she is working in the ways you would wish her to, and using the most effective methods of teaching and behaviour management.

Methods of observation and monitoring

Let's compare monitoring your TA's work with how you monitor your pupils' work. Look back at the notes you made about the ways in which you monitor how well your pupils are working and how well they understand what is expected of them. If you did not make an actual list, you may wish to do that now, so that you can apply your thinking to how you supervise your TA. One of the useful ways of doing this would be to divide your paper into columns. In the left-hand column, list the ways in which you monitor your pupils' work; in the right-hand column, make a note of whether this method could work for monitoring your TA's work. Or use the list you made previously and add a third column to the right.

Ways of monitoring pupil work and performance	Why you do it and what it tells you	Could this method work for monitoring your TAs?
		✓ or X

You can just place a tick (✓) in the right-hand column if you feel that the method of monitoring pupils also applies to TAs, and a cross (X) if you feel that it does not. In the box we have listed some of the monitoring methods that we think are applicable to both pupil and TA work. If you have not included those items in your list, think about them and see whether you think they could work for you and your TA.

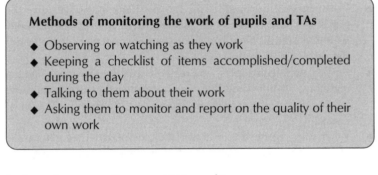

Methods of monitoring the work of pupils and TAs

◆ Observing or watching as they work
◆ Keeping a checklist of items accomplished/completed during the day
◆ Talking to them about their work
◆ Asking them to monitor and report on the quality of their own work

So how do *you* monitor your TA's work?

As you compare your assessment of pupils' achievements, and your assessment of your TA's work, no doubt you will have noted some areas that are *not* the same for monitoring TAs. What are those areas? Make a note of them in the box.

Ways I monitor my TAs that are different from the way I monitor pupils.

_____

_____

_____

_____

It would be important to note here that when you monitor your pupils' work, you are checking against a standard of some sort – curriculum objectives or levels (including those required for passing external exams), reading age or other age-appropriate behaviours, targets set by the LEA, the school, or by you for your classroom or for an individual child. These are predetermined benchmarks or targets you have set, and hopefully discussed with your pupils so that they know what is expected of them. A good example of this is Year 11 pupils sitting mock GCSE exams.

◆ You will have already discussed the syllabus and the requirements with them, and taught the necessary material, so they have a sense of the benchmark and what they are aiming for.

◆ When they sit the mock exam, the questions themselves give the pupils feedback on how well prepared they are – if the questions seem too difficult, they know they've got some work to do before the actual GCSE exam.

◆ As you mark their papers, you see how well they have handled the questions, so you know how well prepared they are – and how much work you have to do to finish preparing them for the actual exam.

◆ When they receive their mark for the mock exam, they get a sense of where they are in relation to the benchmark set for passing their GCSEs.

Reflect and apply

What benchmarks do you think there are for the work your TA does? How does she become aware of those benchmarks or the standard of work expected of her? Take a minute to think about this, and reflect on what you do to identify standards of work for your TA.

_____

_____

_____

_____

There are many ways in which you can set standards for your TA, and her job description is the first place to start in outlining the range and scope of the work you expect her to do. We discussed the need for detailed role assignment in Chapter 2, so in this way you can also provide a sense of the standard expected. There are also national standards for TAs' work, especially the National Occupational Standards (NOS) and the standards for HLTAs. Even if your TA does not have HLTA status, or is not applying for it, the HLTA standards do offer a useful list of possible TA responsibilities and the level at which those responsibilities should be carried out, so we will look at both of those sets of standards. Both the NOS and the HLTA standards can be downloaded from the Teacher Development Agency (TDA) website, with details in the Appendix.

The National Occupational Standards

'best practice expectations [comprising] the factors which together can be used to recognize competent performance, and include the knowledge and understanding which underpins successful performance.'

Local Government National Training Organization (LGNTO)

National Occupational Standards

The NOS for teaching/classroom assistants were developed by the LGNTO and were designed for use across the UK to ensure consistency and transferability of qualifications for TAs. They relate to the work of TAs with all different types of roles and all age groups. They are what the LGNTO called 'best practice expectations' (see above).

They form the basis of National Vocational Qualifications (NVQs) and SVQs (the Scottish equivalent). They have also been recommended for teachers as a basis for determining the CPD needs of TAs. There are also NOS for early years workers, play workers, youth workers, school administrators and bursars. Most recently, the TDA has revised and expanded the NOS for TAs and renamed them NOS for Supporting Teaching and Learning in Schools (STL). These revised standards have superceded the NOS for TAs, but the originals remain valid. Some of the salient features for your work as a supervisor are:

◆ The NOS consist of Units of Competence, each of which covers a discrete area of responsibility (you will find all of the Units listed in the box); there are 69 units in the NOS for supporting teaching and learning.

◆ Each Unit consists of a number of elements, for which there are performance criteria, and expected knowledge and understanding. This makes the NOS particularly valuable for determining and providing CPD for your TA.

Full details can be found on the TDA website (details in the Appendix).

You can see from the list in the box that many of the units would apply directly to your TA's role. There are also units of particular interest to your supervisory role and collaboration with your TA, including: STL21 'Support the development and effectiveness of work teams'; and STL62 'Develop and maintain working relationships with other practitioners'. The second box provides details of some of the standards relating to these units.

National Occupational Standards for Supporting Teaching and Learning – unit titles

STL1   Provide support for learning activities
STL2   Support children's development
STL3   Help to keep children safe
STL4   Contribute to positive relationships
STL5   Provide effective support for your colleagues
STL6   Support literacy and numeracy activities
STL7   Support the use of ICT for teaching and learning
STL8   Use information and communication technology to support pupils' learning
STL9   Observe and report on pupil performance
STL10 Support children's play and learning
STL11 Contribute to supporting bilingual/multilingual pupils
STL12 Support a child with disabilities or special educational needs
STL13 Contribute to moving and handling individuals
STL14 Support individuals during therapy sessions
STL15 Support children and young people's play
STL16 Provide displays

→ *continued*

STL17 Invigilate tests and examinations

STL18 Support pupils' learning activities

STL19 Promote positive behaviour

STL20 Develop and promote positive relationships

STL21 Support the development and effectiveness of work teams

STL22 Reflect on and develop practice

STL23 Plan, deliver and evaluate teaching and learning activities under the direction of a teacher

STL24 Contribute to the planning and evaluation of teaching and learning activities

STL25 Support literacy development

STL26 Support numeracy development

STL27 Support implementation of the early years curriculum

STL28 Support teaching and learning in a curriculum area

STL29 Observe and promote pupil performance and development

STL30 Contribute to assessment for learning

STL31 Prepare and maintain the learning environment

STL32 Promote the transfer of learning from outdoor experiences

STL33 Provide literacy and numeracy support to enable pupils to access the wider curriculum

STL34 Support gifted and talented pupils

STL35 Support bilingual/multilingual pupils

STL36 Provide bilingual/multilingual support for teaching and learning

STL37 Contribute to the prevention and management of challenging behaviour in children and young people

STL38 Support children with disabilities or SEN and their families

STL39 Support pupils with communication and interaction needs

STL40 Support pupils with cognition and learning needs

STL41 Support pupils with behaviour, emotional and social development needs

STL42 Support pupils with sensory and/or physical needs

STL43 Assist in the administration of medication

→ *continued*

STL44 Work with children and young people with additional requirements to meet their personal support needs

STL45 Promote children's well-being and resilience

STL46 Work with young people to safeguard their welfare

STL47 Enable young people to be active citizens

STL48 Support young people in tackling problems and taking action

STL49 Support children and young people during transitions in their lives

STL50 Facilitate children and young people's learning and development through mentoring

STL51 Contribute to improving attendance

STL52 Support children and families through home visiting

STL53 Lead an extracurricular activity

STL54 Plan and support self-directed play

STL55 Contribute to maintaining pupil records

STL56 Monitor and maintain curriculum resources

STL57 Organize cover for absent colleagues

STL58 Organize and supervise travel

STL59 Escort and supervise pupils on educational visits and out-of-school activities

STL60 Liaise with parents, carers and families

STL61 Provide information to aid policy formation and the improvement of practices and provision

STL62 Develop and maintain working relationships with other practitioners

STL63 Provide leadership for your team

STL64 Provide leadership in your area of responsibility

STL65 Allocate and check work in your team

STL66 Lead and motivate volunteers

STL67 Provide learning opportunities for colleagues

STL68 Support learners by mentoring in the workplace

STL69 Support competence achieved in the workplace

National Occupational Standards for Supporting Teaching and Learning – details of units relating to collaborative work

STL21 Support the development and effectiveness of work teams

Elements: 21.1 Contribute to effective team practice
21.2 Contribute to the development of the work team

This unit is about: Being an effective member of a work team. It involves taking an active role in supporting and developing team effectiveness.

STL62 Develop and maintain working relationships with other practitioners

Elements: 62.1 Maintain working relationships with other practitioners
62.2 Work in partnership with other practitioners

This unit is about: Working effectively with other practitioners by doing what can be done to support their work and using their strengths and expertise to support and develop the individual's working practices and procedures.

In the previous chapter we referred to the importance of determining your TA's skills and abilities in determining her roles. Each TA enters her employment with a set of life experiences that gives her additional attributes. She may also have special gifts or talents, such as the ability to draw or paint. When you use the Standards to assess the work of your TA, remember to include those other considerations, and factor in the things she does particularly well, as well as those areas where she struggles or is less confident. Assessment is not for the purpose of only showing weaknesses. It should first measure strengths. In practical terms you may feel that this makes no difference, but psychologically it is an important distinction.

HLTA standards

Candidates for HLTA status must document the ways in which they meet each of the 33 prescribed standards, which are listed in the box below. As you can see from the list, the standards are divided into:

- professional attributes
- professional knowledge and understanding
- professional skills, including
- planning and expectations
- monitoring and assessment
- teaching and learning activities.

In the *HLTA Candidate Handbook* there is a note under the 'Professional skills' subheading that reads: 'Teaching and learning activities must take place under the direction and supervision of an assigned teacher and in accordance with arrangements made by the headteacher of the school.'

As we have already stated, these are specific requirements for HLTA status, not for all TAs, but they do offer a useful list of possible responsibilities that you and your TA could discuss in terms of accountability and monitoring the quality of her work. In the previous chapter we talked about the importance of indicating the limits of your TA's role. This list would provide a useful focus for discussing what you do *not* expect your TA to take on, as well as what you would expect her to be able to do.

Professional standards for Higher Level Teaching Assistant status

Those awarded HLTA status must demonstrate that they:

Professional attributes

1 have high expectations of children and young people with a commitment to helping them fulfil their potential
2 establish fair, respectful, trusting, supportive and constructive relationships with children and young people
3 demonstrate the positive values, attitudes and behaviour they expect from children and young people
4 communicate effectively and sensitively with children, young people, colleagues, parents and carers
5 recognize and respect the contribution that parents and carers can make to the development and well-being of children and young people
6 demonstrate a commitment to collaborative and cooperative working with colleagues

---

→ *continued*

7 improve their own knowledge and practice including responding to advice and feedback

Professional knowledge and understanding

8 understand the key factors that affect children and young people's learning and progress

9 know how to contribute to effective personalized provision by taking practical account of diversity

10 have sufficient understanding of their area(s) of expertise to support the development, learning and progress of children and young people

11 have achieved a nationally recognized qualification at level 2 or above in English/literacy and Mathematics/numeracy

12 know how to use ICT to support their professional activities

13 know how statutory and non-statutory frameworks for the school curriculum relate to the age and ability ranges of the learners they support

14 understand the objectives, content and intended outcomes for the learning activities in which they are involved

15 know how to support learners in accessing the curriculum in accordance with the SEN code of practice and disabilities legislation

16 know how other frameworks that support the development and well-being of children and young people impact upon their practice

Professional skills

Planning and expectations

17 use their area(s) of expertise to contribute to the planning and preparation of learning activities

18 use their area(s) of expertise to plan their role in learning activities

19 devise clearly structured activities that interest and motivate learners and advance their learning

→ *continued*

20 plan how they will support the inclusion of the children and young people in the learning activities

21 contribute to the selection and preparation of resources suitable for children and young people's interests and abilities.

Monitoring and assessment

22 monitor learners' responses to activities and modify the approach accordingly

23 monitor learners' progress in order to provide focused support and feedback

24 support the evaluation of learners' progress using a range of assessment techniques

25 contribute to maintaining and analysing records of learners' progress

Teaching and learning activities

26 use effective strategies to promote positive behaviour

27 recognize and respond appropriately to situations that challenge equality of opportunity

28 use their ICT skills to advance learning

29 advance learning when working with individuals

30 advance learning when working with small groups

31 advance learning when working with whole classes without the presence of the assigned teacher

32 organize and manage learning activities in ways that keep learners safe

33 direct the work, where relevant, of other adults in supporting learning

Setting priorities for improvement

So far in this chapter we have looked at why you monitor the quality of the TA as she works alongside you or as your deputy. We have also briefly considered how you can monitor the quality of her work. We have discussed the standards for excellence that have been established for TAs, particularly the NOS and the standards for HLTA status. In the remainder of the chapter, we will discuss setting priorities for improvement.

So once you have monitored your TA's work, what then? What is your next step as her supervisor? If you have monitored her work, you will have found many areas in which she has considerable strengths. But you no doubt will also have found areas in which she needs assistance and could improve the ways she works.

Setting goals

Here are some guidelines you will find useful as you engage in this process:

- Make sure you engage your TA in the process of selecting areas for improvement – this should not be imposed on her by you, but should be a negotiated agreement between the two of you and should focus on areas that appeal to her as well as to you – for personal and/or professional reasons.
- Be very specific about what you want to improve – choose a well-defined area. For example, rather than choosing to *improve behaviour management,* you should focus on something as small and discrete as *using rewards to encourage good behaviour or using a variety of ways to express approval.* Like teaching, behaviour management is far too large an aspect of the classroom to tackle all at once and consists of many sub-skills, each of which you can – and should – work on individually.
- Choose only one or two areas to focus on at a time – trying to improve *all teaching and learning skills,* for example, is much too broad a goal; aim for something manageable. Once you have accomplished that you can easily move on to the next area. Prioritize a specific aspect and dedicate your efforts to improving that aspect until you see progress. Then you can move on to the next area of priority.
- Always put your goals in writing. Studies have shown that setting a goal without putting it in writing drastically reduces the chances of success.
- Failure does not always mean that you did something wrong in your goal setting or implementation. It may just mean that the time you allotted for achieving your goals was insufficient. Review the process you went through before setting the goal again.
- Put your written goals in a common place where you can both refer to them on a daily basis. *If they are out of sight, they will soon be out of mind.*

◆ Celebrate each small success along the way. When a goal is achieved, take a few minutes – or a lunchtime – to indulge in a small celebration of your joint accomplishments.

Where to start?
Goals that work are a result of:

◆ identifying expectations
◆ determining measure of success
◆ holding effective conversations about the process.

So where is the best place to start? The best place is a conversation between you and your TA. To facilitate the discussion, the following should be helpful:

◆ a copy of your TA's job description – always a great place to start!
◆ the TA standards noted in the text above
◆ any specific work information, e.g. the teaching handbook for the specific area of the curriculum your TA may be working on, or individual plans to meet the needs of particular pupils she works with.

This is a great time to clarify expectations, ask questions and acknowledge the special skills and talents of your TA. And the last and perhaps most important element of the process is to capture the results of the conversation in writing. Keep notes!

Tips for effective goal setting
One commonly used model to help with the goal setting process is the use of 'SMART' goals, that is, goals which are:

S = Specific
M = Measurable
A = Attainable
R = Realistic
T = Timely

Let's look at each of these. You can use them as a guide to help you and your TA develop the goals she will want to follow and you will use for the evaluation or monitoring process. Table 3.1 provides a format for you to consider the practical application of this framework.

Table 3.1. An example of SMART goal setting

Specific	Goals should be straightforward and emphasize what you want to happen. Specifics help us to focus on our efforts and clearly define what we are going to do. Use action words that you can see/show rather than 'thinking' words that can't be seen and measured.	Exactly *what* you are going to do?
Measurable	Establish concrete criteria for measuring each goal. If you can't measure it, you can't assess it. Goals must be measurable to determine success. Set goals with measurable progress – so you can see the change occur. Include a target date.	(Example: Read more vs. read three chapters in the pupils History text by Friday)
Attainable	Goals that are too great will be difficult to reach. Set them in smaller, attainable steps. The goal needs to be challenging, but not impossible to reach. It should feel possible to accomplish it. The feeling of success with the achievement of smaller steps motivates one to continue on to bigger successes.	
Realistic	Realistic means that training to achieve the skills will be available; that the TA's goal fits with the goals of the teacher, pupils and overall school goals. A realistic goal may challenge the TA, but it should not discourage her. As the teacher, you can work with the TA to develop a plan or a way of getting there that makes the goal realistic.	(Example: Take accurate data on a target pupil's on-task behaviour during the history lesson)
Timely	Set a time for the goal to be completed. Putting an end point on the goal gives a clear target to work towards. There is no urgency in meeting the goal if no time has been set; setting an end point makes it feel less like an endless, lifelong pursuit!	(Examples: Friday of next week, in three months, by the end of the term.)

SMART goals are: Specific
                            Measurable
                            Attainable
                            Realistic
                            Timely

It is important to be upfront with your TA so that she understands that she and her work will be monitored. If it is an expectation for her, she will not be surprised and she will know she must work towards the job description and goals established for her employment. Help her see this as an opportunity to learn the things she can do to support pupils in their learning. You will notice that among the HLTA standards there are two in the 'attributes' category that apply here:

Standard 6 demonstrate a commitment to collaborative and co-operative working with colleagues

Standard 7 improve their own knowledge and practice including responding to advice and feedback

You can set the example by showing your TA what you are doing to improve your own practice. This may include attending professional development training, reading professional books, membership of professional organizations etc. But improvement and goal setting can also be part of your daily vocabulary as you go about your work. You can make a point of saying to your TA such things as, 'I've promised myself that I'll be more positive about Tom's behaviour. So I'm going to see if I can find three good things to say to him before break this morning.'

Chapter summary

In this chapter we have been looking at accountability. As a teacher with one or more TAs in your classroom, you must be accountable for their supervision, and they are accountable not only to you and the pupils, but to the expectation that their work will meet a certain standard. You may choose to couch this in the official language of the NOS, or you may set out your expectations in a less formal way. As you monitor your TA's work, you can identify areas where she can improve – indeed, she can help identify areas in which she feels that she needs to improve – and you can play a major role in helping her to set goals. You can also monitor and support her as she progresses in the small steps that will lead her towards achievement of the larger goals. In the next chapter we will be looking at ways in which you can provide or facilitate professional development opportunities for your TA.

4 | Providing Continuous Professional Development

In the previous chapters we have already discussed:

◆ how you delegate responsibilities to your TA
◆ the need for your TA to be assigned roles according to her level of skill.

In this chapter we look at how your TA can develop additional skills in order to perform well in the responsibilities she has been assigned, and how important it is for you to encourage this development as her supervisor. We also look at the importance of treating your TA as an adult learner, and the ways in which you can make resources available to her. In addition we look at some of the popular theories of learning, particularly social constructivism, to see what insights they have to offer on how to provide effective professional development.

What is CPD?

The General Teaching Council for Wales (GTCW) gives this definition of CPD:

Continuing Professional Development encompasses all formal and informal learning which enables teachers to improve their own practice.

The TDA defines CPD as:

... reflective activity designed to improve an individual's attributes, knowledge, understanding and skills. It supports individual needs and improves professional practice.

In 2002 the GTCW published the document 'Continuing Professional Development'. In it, the Council states:

> In an ever changing world, teachers need continually to update their professional skills to ensure that teaching continues to be of high quality and education standards continue to improve. As well as contributing to school improvement, the provision of CPD opportunities can assist in teachers developing themselves as reflective practitioners.

The Welsh Department for Children, Education, Lifelong Learning and Skills (DCELLS) has stated that CPD is an entitlement for all teachers in Wales. Although this document is addressing the need for teachers to have opportunities for professional development, the logic for that development – 'to ensure that teaching continues to be of high quality and education standards continue to improve' – certainly holds good for TAs. One of the basic assumptions of this book is that TAs affect the quality of what schools offer. Logically then, professional development is as essential for TAs as it is for teachers. The DCELLS document is aimed primarily at senior management teams in schools. However it also offers useful principles for teachers who supervise TAs, because we can take the idea one step further by saying that as teachers are enabled to improve their own practice, so can TAs improve their practices when providing support to teachers. When TAs direct their efforts to continual development of their skills, they offer their support to high quality teaching, which in turn supports pupils in reaching high education standards. When both teachers and TAs strive for continual improvement, together they support continual school improvement.

A 2005 DfES document noted the increase in TAs in schools and the key role they play as schools implement workforce reforms set out in the National Agreement for Raising Standards and Tackling Workload. 'The effective management of teaching assistants to improve standards in Literacy and Mathematics' states:

> Evidence shows that teaching assistants are more likely to have the skills and knowledge to support pupil learning effectively if they have received appropriate induction training and continuing professional development.
>
> Training for teaching assistants should:

◆ be planned, systematic and cumulative;
◆ be identified in the school development plan and individual performance management portfolios;
◆ relate to identified national, school and personal priorities;
◆ over time, contain a balance of general and subject-specific training, including developing subject knowledge;
◆ be monitored for impact and effectiveness;
◆ include opportunities for teachers and teaching assistants to undertake joint professional development within and beyond the school.

In November 2007, the EPPI-Centre at the University of London's Institute of Education published a report entitled 'Working with adults: How training and professional development activities impact on Teaching Assistants' classroom practice'. (Details of where to access a copy of this report online can be found in the Appendix.) As the title suggests, the report looked at the impact of training and CPD on TAs' work. This included both primary and secondary phases.

The report reviews only published articles and training programmes, but it is interesting to note that the initial question through which the researchers looked at the published literature was: What is the impact (both measured and perceived) of training on primary and secondary TAs and their ability to support pupils' learning and engagement? More specifically, the researchers also asked: What is the impact of award-bearing training on paid primary and secondary TAs in mainstream schools?

The authors of the study drew some unfortunate conclusions that are not likely to be a surprise to many TAs. They found:

◆ TA training is patchy and its impact is little understood.

◆ Policy on training for TAs has not been coordinated, despite significant policy developments relating to TAs in recent years. Programmes exist in the UK, USA and elsewhere, but these are relatively uncoordinated, despite such initiatives as the Specialist Training Assistant programme in the UK and No Child Left Behind in the USA.

◆ Where available, training programmes can be effective in raising awareness, in developing TAs' confidence and subject knowledge, including their instructional skills; but exactly how these impacts are achieved is not clear.

Establishing the effectiveness of TAs is difficult. Indeed the subject of teacher effectiveness has been highly controversial, with many teachers objecting to the use of league tables and results of formal examinations as measures of their ability to teach. There are so many factors that impact pupil achievement, and the teacher (or TA) is literally only one of those factors, albeit a very important one. Nevertheless, we can surely agree with the last point made in the EPPI-Centre report that 'training ... can be effective in raising awareness, in developing TAs' confidence and subject knowledge'. Our suggestions here for CPD are based on the assumption that this is a justifiable claim.

Reflect and apply

Think for a moment about your own professional development. What do you typically do to access CPD? How do you find out about it in the first place? What type of CPD do you usually engage in – how do you decide what professional development opportunities to take up and what makes CPD appealing? What have you learned from recently attended CPD events or opportunities?

When you think about the training offered to your TA, do the same conditions apply? How do TAs find out about courses or training opportunities? And what would motivate your TAs to take up opportunities for CPD?

You may find it interesting to know that some years ago we surveyed some four hundred TAs who were attending various conferences and other training in the UK, the USA and Canada. We asked them to tell us what motivated them to attend training. The reason that they most frequently listed was, they wanted to learn so they could be better able to help pupils. The second most common reason was, because a teacher or head had made a recommendation that they should attend (which suggests that you may have more influence than you think). Almost last on the list of reasons was any mention of pay or other financial incentives. Do you think the results of this study would also apply to your TA? What do you think motivates your TA to want to attend training or take up opportunities for CPD? You might ask and see what she has to say.

Treating your TA as an adult learner

You may have acquired your teaching qualifications in your early 20s, perhaps straight from school and 'A' levels. Or you may have returned to study as a mature student, perhaps as a change in career or after family or other commitments. Your TA will almost certainly be a mature student – the majority of TAs are. As adults we are accustomed to being – and being thought of as – competent and able. We may not feel entirely confident in what we do, but we can usually find our comfort zone in our work and in our personal lives. Then as the work demands, and as we feel brave enough, we may stretch ourselves to learn new skills or tackle new aspects of the job. We take the risk of being a learner. This can typically be very fulfilling, to see our skills gradually growing and developing. When you begin the process of deliberately and systematically leading the learning of your TA, you are making that sort of learning very open and explicit. There may be some risk in taking the lead. Your TA may certainly feel that she is taking a risk in engaging in professional development activities. A risk not taken may indeed be a missed opportunity. However, be aware that as an adult learner, your TA may:

◆ feel concerned about her lack of formal qualifications and therefore her ability to learn
◆ be aware of the length of time since she was last studying and wonder whether she can pick up again from where she left off
◆ feel anxious when she thinks of learning, especially if her own experiences of school were not altogether positive
◆ be reluctant to ask questions, fearing that they may reveal her ignorance
◆ be unsure about what to expect of formal professional develop-

ment opportunities, and therefore insecure or reluctant to take them up.

These are common reactions for adult learners, especially those who have been absent from study for some time.

'The dangers of life are infinite, and among them is safety.'

– Goethe

Your TA will want to be safe, but help her to see that learning requires some risks and you are there to support her learning. With support, she can develop the skills to become a lifelong learner.

Learning theory

Over the course of your career as a teacher, and during your training for becoming a teacher, you have no doubt come across a variety of learning theories and theorists who proposed models of how children learn and gain in understanding. Among the most influential education theorists from the twentieth century are Jean Piaget (1896–1980), Lev Vygotsky (1896–1934) and Jerome Bruner (1915–). A brief summary of some of the main ideas proposed by each of these theorists can be found in the box below. The combination of ideas they proposed has come to be known as Social Constructivism. Although these are theories of how children learn, they also offer some useful insights into adult learning and the principles you might bear in mind when offering learning opportunities to your TA. These are the four principle ideas of Social Constructivism:

◆ Principle 1: The learning process is one of interactions between the known and the unknown, i.e. what is to be learned
◆ Principle 2: Learning is a social process, involving interaction with other people; this interaction allows for sharing of knowledge and understanding
◆ Principle 3: Learning is influenced by context, but may not transfer easily from one context to another
◆ Principle 4: Metacognition – awareness of one's own learning – is an important part of the learning process.

If you would like to read more about Social Constructivism, the book by Medwell and Wray, *Letts QTS Guide: Teaching English in Primary Schools*, (details in the Appendix) will provide you with a very readable summary.

Let's consider the implications of these principles to your work with your TA as an adult learner.

Principle 1: The learning process is one of interactions between the known and what is to be learned

Three things come to mind here:

1) the importance of the learner being aware of what he or she already knows
2) the need for the teacher to ascertain what the learner already knows before introducing new ideas or information
3) the need for the teacher to make links for the learner between the known and the new

Principle 2: Learning is a social process, involving interaction with other people; this interaction allows for sharing of knowledge and understanding

Two things emerge from this principle:

1) solitude is not the best learning situation – learning needs company
2) the mere presence of another adult is not enough – the two adults need to be interacting (discussing, working together) for the best learning to occur

Principle 3: Learning is influenced by context, but may not transfer easily from one context to another

This principle suggests two things:

1) the need to be sensitive to the context in which learning is taking place – ensuring that it is appropriate to the learner's cultural/ linguistic background, and that it closely resembles the context in which the new learning will be used
2) you may need to help your learner to generalize principles learned in one context so that she understands whether/how they apply to other contexts or situations

Principle 4: Metacognition – awareness of one's own learning – is an important part of the learning process

This suggests that you need to help your learner:

1) understand the learning that is taking place, as well as the ways in which she is learning
2) appreciate the extent and limits of her knowledge/understanding – to acknowledge gaps and remain aware of the need for additional learning.

We will talk more about this in Chapter 5 (Reflective Practice).

Reflect and apply

Take a moment to think about these principles and how you could apply them to your work with your TA. What do you already do that addresses these principles? What could you change about what you do to more closely address these principles?

As we proceed through the remainder of the chapter – and indeed through the rest of the book – we will be revisiting the principles from a variety of perspectives.

Some of the influential ideas proposed by Jean Piaget (1896–1980)

1. Understanding is actively constructed or created through the learner's interaction with his or her environment; as children play they test out their theories of how their world works.
2. As children interact with their environment, they develop 'schemata' – that is, mental pictures of how things are; they assimilate new experiences into existing schemata, and modify or restructure these mental pictures as new experiences dictate, by a process Piaget called 'accommodation'.

→ *continued*

3. Children's cognitive development passes through a series of stages: sensori-motor (learning through movement), pre-operational (based largely on intuition rather than logic), concrete operational (thinking becomes more logical) and formal operational (increasing ability to think logically and use abstract symbols and concepts).

Some of the influential ideas proposed by Lev Vygotsky (1896–1934)

1. The use of cultural or psychological tools – in the same way that humans use physical tools to enhance their physical work, we use a variety of psychological tools (symbols, numbers, pictures, language) to help us deal with our world.
2. The interrelationship between language and thought, with thought being internalized language, and language ability therefore being crucial to the ability to think.
3. Learning takes place in a social context, and therefore other people are important in the process of learning.
4. Zone of proximal development – the difference between what is already known and the next step in learning, what a child can already do and what he or she needs to progress to, with learning facilitated by a more expert other (adult or peer).
5. Metacognition as a stage in the learning process – that is, not only knowing something, but knowing that we know and being aware of how we came to know it.
6. The importance of play, as it allows children to rehearse what they already know, try out new ideas and take risks in the safe environment of make-believe.

Some of the influential ideas proposed by Jerome Bruner (1915–)

1. Children move through a sequence of stages in their development, and they continue to operate in these different ways even into adulthood. The stages are: enactive (learning by doing), iconic (using pictures, diagrams and numbers to help the thinking process) and symbolic (working with abstract concepts and symbolism).

→ *continued*

2. Knowledge is actively constructed through the learner's experiences. In connection with this idea, Bruner developed the theory of a 'spiral curriculum', building on previous knowledge and understanding and making deliberate connections with prior learning.
3. Both language and culture play a critical part in learning.
4. The need for 'scaffolding' in the learning process – that is, support by an adult (or more expert peer) for when the child is faced with a learning challenge.

Making professional resources available

One of the ways in which you can assist your TA to develop professionally is to make professional resources available to her. Your TA may well belong to a professional organization – mostly likely a union – but typically that will not be a teaching union that provides resources relating directly to the job of being a TA. Resources you can make available to her might include:

♦ Professional journals to which you subscribe as a teacher. These may be subject-based (for example, if your subject area is maths, you may be a member of the Association of Maths Teachers, and receive their publication *Mathematics Teaching*) or they may be more generally related to teaching and learning. As you receive and read these publications, make a note of items that you think would be of particular interest and use to your TA, and then make sure you pass them on to her. This selective filtering of information is likely to be less intimidating for your TA than just handing over the publication and leaving it to her to find something useful.

♦ Check whether your school subscribes to journals or magazines; if they do, let your TA know where they are kept (usually on a shelf in the staff room) and that she can make use of them.

♦ When you come across articles or studies relating to the role of TAs, share them with your TA and talk about the relevance of the study to her work.

♦ Talk to the Head and school secretary and let them know that if any information comes to the school about training or resources for TAs, you would like to see it, to pass it on to your TA. When mailings come to schools – particularly large secondary schools –

without a named person on the address label, the secretary may not know whom to forward it to, so useful material can easily be lost in the system (or binned!).

◆ Teachers TV – which you are hopefully familiar with and have made use of – now has resources for TAs, and you will find details of where to access these in the Appendix.

◆ 'Teaching Ideas' is another online resource for TAs, providing free ideas, resources and activities for teaching (www.teachingideas. co.uk).

These are tangible resources you can share with your TA, but there are also human resources available to you both:

◆ If you have a teacher colleague who you know is particularly adept at using teaching methods that would be suitable for your TA, you may wish to approach him or her and ask if your TA can spend some time observing his/her teaching. Although few of us like to be watched as we teach, the implied compliment in this request should help to avoid a refusal. If your TA is to observe in another teacher's classroom, it is most important that you discuss the observation beforehand so that you can guide her on what to observe and how to record her observations. Of course, the discussion you engage in should not focus on the teacher as such, but on the teaching. If your colleague is willing, it would also be useful for your TA to be able to discuss the observation with him or her.

◆ Observe your TA as she works with an individual child or small group of pupils and discuss your observations with her. If you can combine this with a brief discussion prior to the observation to agree on the focus of the observation, the discussion can be more specific and target areas you have already identified as being currently important. An observation sheet where you can make objective notes of what you see and hear will help to make the discussions and the observation even more focused.

◆ Encourage your TA to observe you while she completes an observation sheet similar to the one you use when you observe her. If she observes you first and has the same focus for the observation as you will have when you observe her, you will be able to provide her with a model of how you would like her to carry out particular tasks, or how certain teaching strategies can be used. Again, this observation should be paired with discussion –

prior to the observation to clarify what she is focusing on, and after the observation to discuss what she has observed.

It is useful and important to keep track of these types of professional development activities that have taken place. In a later chapter we will discuss the importance of keeping evidence of your TA's CPD and suggest ways to support developing a portfolio of CPD activities.

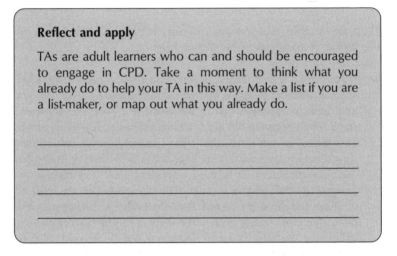

Reflect and apply

TAs are adult learners who can and should be encouraged to engage in CPD. Take a moment to think what you already do to help your TA in this way. Make a list if you are a list-maker, or map out what you already do.

The 2004 DfES document 'Excellence and enjoyment: Learning and teaching in the primary years' sets out principles for learning and teaching. These relate to pupil learning, but offer useful guidelines for adult learning as well – that is, the professional development that you engage in together with your TA. The principles are:

◆ set high expectations and give every learner confidence that they can succeed
◆ establish what learners already know, and build on it
◆ structure and pace the learning experience to make it challenging and enjoyable
◆ inspire learning through passion for the subject
◆ make individuals active partners in their learning
◆ develop learning skills and personal qualities.

You will find more detail on each of these principles in the box.

Principles for learning and teaching

Set high expectations and give every learner confidence that they can succeed:

◆ demonstrate a commitment to every learner's success, making them feel included, valued and secure
◆ raise learners' aspirations and the effort they put into learning.

Establish what learners already know and build on it:

◆ set clear and appropriate learning goals, making every learning experience count
◆ create secure foundations for subsequent learning.

Structure and pace the learning experience to make it challenging and enjoyable:

◆ use teaching methods that reflect the material to be learned, match the maturity of the learners and their learning preferences, and involve high levels of time on task
◆ make creative use of a range of learning opportunities, within and beyond the classroom.

Inspire learning through passion for the subject:

◆ bring the subject alive
◆ make it relevant to learners' wider goals and concerns.

Make individuals active partners in their learning:

◆ build respectful teacher–learner relationships that take learners' views and experience fully into account
◆ use assessment for learning to help learners assess their work, reflect on how they learn and inform subsequent planning and practice.

Develop learning skills and personal qualities:

◆ develop the ability to think systematically, manage information, learn from others and help others learn
◆ develop confidence, self-discipline and an understanding of the learning process.

For a fuller version see: www.standards.dfes.gov.uk/personalisedlearning/five/teachinglearning/

'Excellence and enjoyment: Learning and teaching in the primary years' also suggests a cycle for school improvement that lends itself well to the cycle of reflection, evaluation and professional development you can engage in with your TA.

Perhaps the most useful – certainly the most accessible – forms of CPD that you provide for your TA will be the day-to-day on-the-job training opportunities you take advantage of as they arise. However, you can also point your TA in the direction of more formal CPD opportunities. A useful source of information on formal qualifications available for TAs can be found on the TDA website (details in the Appendix). Under the heading 'The support staff framework' there are lists of a wide variety of possible qualifications and training schemes from Level 1 (the equivalent of pre-GCSE) through to Level 7 (Masters degree). They are also listed under the variety of roles or job titles TAs may have – Cover supervisor, Behaviour Support, Early Years, Special Needs etc. Table 4.1 shows a selection for TAs or those providing bilingual support.

The DCSF website provides information on the early years Foundation Stage. Under the title 'Key elements of effective

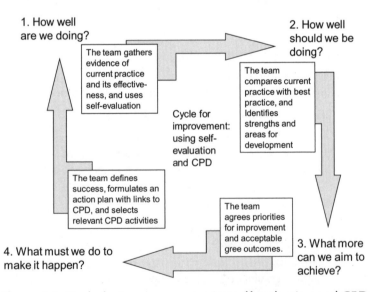

Figure 4.1. Cycle for improvement using self-evaluation and CPD

(Adapted from 'Cycle for School Improvement. Excellence and enjoyment: Learning and teaching in the primary years'. DfES, 2004.)

Table 4.1. A selection of formal qualifications available to those working as Teaching Assistants or Bilingual Support

	Teaching Assistant/Bilingual Support
Level 1	Better Reading Partners
	Foundation award in caring for children
	Helping in Schools
	National award in working with children
Level 2	Apprenticeship for teaching assistants
	Award in using ICT as a tool for learning
	Award/certificate in support work in school (pilot)
	Certificate for teaching assistants
	GCSE subject
	NVQ for teaching assistants
Level 3	'A' level
	Advanced Apprenticeship for TAs
	Award/certificate/diploma in support work in schools (pilot)
	Certificate for TAs
	Certificate in ESOL subject support
	Certificate in off-site safety management
	Certificate of professional development in work with children and young people
	NVQ for teaching assistants
Level 4	Certificate in FE teaching stage 1
	Certificate in supporting learning in primary schools
	HLTA training and/or assessment
Level 5	Foundation degree for TAs
	Higher National Certificate/Diploma in advanced practice in work with children and families
Level 6	Degree in education or any subject
Level 7	MA in education
	Post Graduate Diploma in Education Studies
	Post Graduate Certificate in Education/Graduate Teacher Programme

practice', there is also a potential structure for determining the CPD needs of your TA, especially if you work in the early years Foundation Stage (in England) or Foundation Phase (in Wales).

The DCFS recommends that TAs in England should undergo induction training soon after starting their employment. This is the responsibility of the LEA but the training should be based on materials provided by the DCFS. There is no requirement for Welsh LEAs to use the induction materials provided, although it is recommended that new

TAs appointed to schools in Wales be provided with some form of induction training. However the induction materials are available for download from the TDA website (details in the Appendix). Topics covered in the induction training materials include: behaviour management, child protection, ICT in teaching and learning, SEN, inclusion and understanding how children learn. As such, they offer useful information for your TA, which you can offer as reading material for her and use as a discussion focus together.

The context for learning

Jean Lave and Etienne Wenger in their 2003 book *Situated Learning: Legitimate Peripheral Participation* (details in the Appendix) discuss the importance of the context in which learning takes place. They suggest that learning of any sort is really a social process, and they make a couple of important points that are interesting for this discussion of TAs and CPD:

◆ that understanding and learning develop best in social situations where there is interaction with others
◆ that the best sort of learning is not to do with acquiring a particular knowledge set, but rather acquiring skills by engaging in a social process
◆ that communities learn, not just individuals; where one individual within the group grows in understanding the whole group benefits as the teacher learns by teaching
◆ that learning can occur whenever there is one individual who is more skilled than another.

Lave and Wenger discuss the importance of apprenticeship – not just the historical model of the apprentice articled to a master and learning by doing – but of a newcomer joining in and becoming more expert. They use the term 'peripheral' to describe the apprentice's participation, but this does not denote that the learner is outside the circle or marginalized in any way. They talk about this peripherality being empowering, because even a newcomer (or someone less expert) can participate and contribute to what is happening with increasing intensity as his or her skills and understanding build. But they do warn that peripherality can be disempowering if the expert (and that's you, the teacher) limits the apprentice's participation unnecessarily and keeps them out on the edge. Because you have so much to do, you know the need to delegate responsibilities according to your TA's skills and knowledge, and to add to those responsibilities as her skills and knowledge increase. This suggests a fine balance is needed between limiting a TA's role based on her current skills and allowing her to participate as widely as possible in the teaching/learning process so that she gains more experience. There should be a sense of growing involvement and movement from peripheral to full participation.

Chapter summary

In this chapter we have been considering some of the ways in which you can facilitate for your TA the process of CPD. As a context for this CPD, we have taken a brief look at some of the main principles of social constructivism, and of the notion of legitimate peripheral participation. While social constructivism has been proposed and widely adopted in relation to children's learning, the principles translate easily into the arena of adult learning, and also link well to legitimate peripheral participation, which takes account of the social context for adult learning, as your TA serves her apprenticeship with you.

5 | Reflective Practice

The term 'reflective practitioner' has been part of the education vocabulary in the UK for some years now. Many researchers have noted that every minute of every hour that teachers teach, they are faced with complex decisions concerning the delivery of curriculum content and appropriate teaching strategies, as well as considerations such as fairness, democracy and other competing ethical claims. With so many serious, daily decisions to take, reflection is vital to a teacher's determination of how effective his or her teaching may be. Teachers have been encouraged to use reflection to become more aware of what they do and why they do it. Awareness is the first step towards change and change is our business as teachers. But much of our focus has historically been on changing children's behaviour – both their social and their learning behaviours – rather than on our own behaviour as teachers and managers of the learning environment. Only recently has reflective practice become part of the vocabulary for TAs – largely as Higher Education courses specifically for TAs (such as the Foundation Degree) have become more widely available.

One of the particularly well-known thinkers in the field of reflective practice is Donald A. Schon. In his 1987 book *Educating the Reflective Practitioner*, he talks about reflection *on action* (which occurs after the event) as well as reflection *in action* (which occurs during the event), or what he refers to as 'thought turning back on itself, thinking what we're doing as we're doing it'. These are the types of reflection that you engage in daily as a teacher:

◆ thinking on your feet and adapting what you do according to the dynamics of the class you are teaching (reflection in action)
◆ sitting down with a cuppa at the end of the day and thinking back over what you accomplished (reflection on action).

In an earlier piece of writing (1983), Schon suggested that reflection is *central to what professionals do*. Reflection in action, or thinking on our feet, involves testing out our ideas and developing or adjusting responses according to what is happening. Reflection on action occurs later, after the event, and allows us to spend more time exploring why we acted as we did, and developing questions and ideas about our activities and practice. In both cases, however, this is what might be termed *content* reflection, as it is largely descriptive:

◆ what happened during that lesson?
◆ how did it happen?
◆ how could it have been done differently?

Reflection on action – looking back at what happened

Reflection in action – reflecting on what is happening as it happens

---

Reflect and apply

Take some time to think about the different types of reflective activities you engage in – whether alone or with someone. These may not have anything to do with the classroom, but could relate to other aspects of your life. What does reflection look like when you engage in it? What are you actually doing when you reflect? Where do you usually engage in reflection? In the bath? On the bus? Take a moment to write down some of your thoughts.

_____

_____

_____

_____

Now consider: What is the product or outcome of your reflective activities? Do you say, 'That didn't go well,' and ditch the activity or idea, or do you use the conclusions you have drawn from your reflection to make changes?

Perhaps some of your most regular reflection activities are conducted informally, as your family sits around the Sunday dinner table and looks back at the week, or forward to the upcoming week, negotiating arrangements and schedules. Or perhaps you sit down with a gardening catalogue, or a DIY manual and plan some house or garden improvements. After all, when you decide which plants to bulb this Autumn, you will not only reflect on what colours you would like and where you would like the bulbs, but probably also think back to last year's plantings and consider how well they worked out in terms of colour scheme, visibility and whether the plants thrived where you put them. As you look back on the week's events with family members and plan for the coming week, you will be considering options, comparing ideas and making judgements based on how well previous arrangements worked etc. Reflection is generally part of our everyday lives, and – whether you engage in it formally or deliberately or not – it forms part of what you do as a teacher.

Reflection vs. critical reflection

In the professional literature, the distinction is made between *reflection* and *critical reflection*. Before we make this distinction and define *critical reflection*, however, it would be useful to consider the ideas of Jack Mezirow, an American university professor specializing in adult learning. His work in the late 1970s is particularly appropriate to this discussion, because he focused his research on adult women returning to education after a break – usually to bring up children – as part of the women's movement in the United States at the time. Out of this research came the idea of learning as transformation (which incidentally is the title of a book written by Mezirow and his colleagues, the details of which are in the Appendix, and which makes interesting reading).

Learning as transformation – or Transformation Theory – centres around the idea of learning as making meaning. As new information comes our way, we try to make sense of it or give it some relevance in our lives. Jean Piaget, the Swiss psychologist, talked about children's learning and used the term *accommodation* to denote that young children constantly try to make sense of their world and of what happens around them. They ascribe meaning to what they experience. However, they may have to adjust their ideas of how the world works as they receive new information and gain new experiences. The new information has to be absorbed into their current understanding, which is obviously then changed in some way by the accommodations they make. As adults we have much more well-established ideas of how the world works, and can become entrenched in those ideas unless we keep an open mind. Or unless we deliberately expose ourselves to learning opportunities, which can provide a wealth of new ideas that we must make sense of in relation to what we already know and believe. So when Mezirow talks about learning as transformation, he is referring primarily to the transformation of our thinking and understanding – our meaning perspectives, or the way we see things. Learning transforms our basic assumptions, which hopefully then influences the way we act. Central to the process of transformative learning, according to Mezirow, is critical reflection. As a teacher, you are faced with problems and dilemmas every day – sometimes you probably feel bombarded by the number of questions and decisions that come your way, each of which must be addressed. Good problem-solving requires critical reflection as you take what you know and revise or adapt it to meet each pupil's unique learning needs, and then reflect on the successfulness of what you have done.

> 'Learning is understood as the process of using a prior interpretation to construe a new or revised interpretation of the meaning of one's experience as a guide to future action.'
> Mezirow, 2000

What is critical reflection?

Critical reflection is considered to be quite distinct from reflection, in that it is reflection that reaches deeper, to the level of challenging your own assumptions. It is not just a matter of describing or revisiting what happened and analysing why; for example:

That Year 8 geography lesson was a mess. I thought they'd remember more about the ecosystems we discussed last term – they weren't really with me on that – and they'd just had a wet breaktime!

It involves questioning what your own beliefs are in relation to the situation, which would involve asking questions such as:

That Year 8 geography lesson was a mess, but what are my expectations of Year 8 geography, especially after a wet breaktime? Do I always have low expectations of that class? Is it because there are so many rowdy boys in there?

Reflection, then, only becomes *critical* reflection when the focus of the reflection is a person's basic assumptions, or meaning perspective. Critical reflection is therefore seen as a means by which personal transformation can take place – it changes us because it requires us to examine and justify our views and what we consider to be 'truth' – or change them according to new information and experiences. There is a clear relationship between reflection on action and reflection in action, but the absence of reflection on meaning perspectives is what distinguishes between these concepts and critical reflection.

'Critical reflection addresses the question of the justification for the very premises on which problems are posed or defined in the first place. We very commonly check our prior learning to confirm that we have correctly proceeded to solve problems, but becoming critically aware of our own presuppositions involves challenging our established and habitual patterns of expectation, the meaning perspectives with which we have made sense out of our encounters with the world, others, and ourselves.' Mezirow, 1990

As we stated earlier, reflection may be an activity that we engage in on a regular basis – in our personal and professional lives – but how often do we reflect *critically*? That is, reflecting deeply enough to question our assumptions, rather than just as a mental review of the activities of the day. Think about this example of questioning assumptions.

Some years ago an LEA advisor visited a school at the request of the Headteacher to talk to staff about ways in which they could change their classrooms to enhance their potential as learning environments. The school had been built in the 1950s and was a fairly standard Ushaped design of that era, with two corridors of identical square classrooms and a grassy quadrangle in between. Each of the classrooms had a wall of windows on one side facing onto the school grounds, but no direct access to the outside. The advisor asked the teachers how they would change their classrooms if there were no limits to what they could do.

After giving them time to think and discuss their ideas, he asked, 'Would you put a fountain in your classroom, or would you plant trees?' The teachers were all dumb-founded. They had been day-dreaming of unlimited supplies of coloured paper, a computer just for their class (there were only two in the whole school at the time), or perhaps some of those nice tessellating tables instead of the old rectangular ones they currently had. And indeed some of them asked, rather indignantly, 'What's the point of day-dreaming about trees or fountains when we have four solid walls, and get complaints from the cleaners if the floor gets wet after we've had an art session?'

The discussion seemed counter-productive to the teachers in the group, because it merely served to emphasize their lack of control over the physical boundaries of their classrooms and the resources available to them. But the advisor's question was a reasonable one in the sense that it challenged the teachers' assumptions about what could be done, even within the physical confines of their classrooms. They were allowing their thinking to be bound by those walls and complaints. Even if they could not have a full-size horse chestnut or weeping willow tree in their classroom, if they could modify or see beyond their current assumptions and think in those larger terms, they might be able to see the possibilities for changing their classrooms for the better, even if it meant scaling down their ideas. The advisor was in a sense telling them that they could have classrooms that looked more like what they really wanted them to be – but not if they persisted with their limited thinking and assumptions.

Thinking outside the classroom walls

We now have initiatives such as the Forest School, which (as the organization's website states) is 'an innovative educational approach to outdoor play and learning'. The stated philosophy of the Forest School organization is to 'encourage and inspire individuals of any age through positive outdoor experiences'. Many schools are adopting a Forest School approach as part of their pedagogy, and some are assigning TAs to attend training and be the school expert. In Wales, the Foundation Phase, and in England the Foundation Stage, require an outdoor component to early years education with encouragement to take all types of lessons outside, not just those typically associated with the outdoors, such as games and the use of large play equipment. To that end, schools in Wales (where the Foundation Phase runs from Nursery through Year 1) must have a supply of outdoor gear so that all children can enjoy a classroom that extends both indoors and outdoors in all weathers. In Scotland the Curriculum for Excellence encourages the use of outdoor learning experiences, with the charity Grounds for Learning providing support to schools in how to make best use of the outdoors. (You can find the Grounds for Learning website in the Appendix.) These types of initiatives stem from the thinking of people who have challenged some of the basic assumptions of the education system to date:

School children only go outdoors at playtime or for games, and
Education takes place within the confines of the classroom or on formal
field-trips.

In a research study conducted with TAs who were enrolled on a Foundation Degree in learning support in 2007, TAs were asked about their perceptions and understanding of reflection and critical reflection. Ann Birch, the Foundation Degree programme director, had encouraged the TAs to engage in reflection during the course, and carried out the study with a view to improving, among other things, their experience of studying at Higher Education level. The study found that TAs understood the meaning of reflection, and when they were asked to articulate their understanding of the term *critical reflection* they suggested that:

◆ critical reflection is about looking back, taking a step back and reflecting on one's experiences
◆ the act of critical reflection includes analysing/commenting on past events, evaluating, learning from experience, examining a topic, agreeing or disagreeing, asking questions and giving reasons for opinions/conclusions, establishing elements of success or faults and weaknesses.

The TAs understood that the *subjects* of reflection could be:

- their own experiences
- elements of successful experiences
- faults or weaknesses
- things others had said or done
- things they had read
- a situation or event
- a topic or subject.

However, what they understood as *critical* reflection was in fact reflection, because it lacked the element of questioning and evaluating their own beliefs or meaning perspectives.

Reflect and apply

This might be a good time to think about some of your own basic assumptions about education. Perhaps you feel that you already have a clear idea of your own philosophy of education, or perhaps you think more in terms of the tasks associated with being a teacher, rather than overarching principles and concepts. Whichever is the case, take a moment to think how you would complete the sentence: *Education means ...* or *Education is ...*

_____

_____

_____

_____

In the box are some of the types of phrases that are commonly bandied about in relation to education. Your reaction to them will say a lot about what you feel education is, and what it is for. But whether you agree or disagree with them, try to dig a little deeper in your thinking. If you agree, try to decide why you agree – what are you assuming by agreeing with the phrase? And if you disagree, try to decide exactly why it is that you disagree – what principle would you propose instead?

Common phrases used in relation to education

◆ a good education will set you up for life
◆ the only person who is educated is the one who has learned how to learn and change (Carl Rogers)
◆ if you want a good job, you need a good education
◆ education improves society
◆ education is not preparation for life; education is life itself (John Dewey)
◆ a good education is another name for happiness (Ann Plato).

If you want to explore your own basic assumptions about education a little further, it would be a good idea to talk with a colleague or friend and ask them for their reactions to those phrases, or ask them to articulate what they think education is. Look back at the last line in the text box: *a good education is another name for happiness*. Does it change your assumptions when you learn that Ann Plato said this in 1841? At the time she was a free, black African American who was a schoolmistress in Hartford, in the American state of Connecticut.

This second part of the 'Reflect and apply' exercise – talking to a colleague or friend – constitutes what Jack Mezirow refers to as *constructive or reflective discourse*: dialogue with another person where ideas and assumptions are aired and tried out. In the previous chapter we referred to Social Constructivism and the work of the Russian psychologist Lev Vygotsky. Vygotsky stressed the importance of language as a vehicle for thinking, and discussion with another person as a means of expanding our thinking. The young child talks to himself as he carries out a task or plays, and his talk parallels his actions. As the child matures, his thinking becomes internalized and this self-talk disappears. In adults it usually reappears in times of stress or when we have to complete a task that is challenging. We read the recipe or directions for assembling flat-pack furniture out loud, because it helps us to keep track of what we need to do. In terms of ideas, when we are obliged to express them out loud it helps crystallize our thinking, and shows us where there are gaps in our understanding.

As we hear another person's views, our views are challenged and perhaps refined. Unfortunately, Mezirow points out, Western culture does not really promote collaborative thinking due to a prevailing notion that there is always a *right* answer. And if there is always a right answer, then opposing or differing views are, by implication, wrong. There are indisputably right and wrong answers to many of life's questions, 2 + 2 is always 4, but for many (perhaps most) of the questions, we might often say, *well it all depends*. And it does depend on:

◆ the individual (what is right for 8-year-old Thomas may not be not right for 10-year-old William, or even 8-year-old George)
◆ the context (your classroom vs. someone else's)
◆ the time (playtime vs. class time, morning vs. afternoon).

... and so on. As a teacher working with a TA, you are well-placed to engage in reflective discourse as you discuss classroom issues. But neither of you should be trying to 'win'. The true purpose of discussion should be to build consensus – to agree on how you will jointly proceed. We might also point out that every discussion you have with your TA does not have to be deeply philosophical. It is perfectly acceptable to review the day's activities or a particular child's behaviour in descriptive terms, because that does help you to remember and focus. But at least some of the reflection you engage in should be *critical* reflection, because only discussion at that level will help you understand some of the events in your classroom in a way that will enable you to work through them towards a better practice.

So let's see how this relates to your own reflective practice and that of your TA. First, let's look at the mentoring you can provide for you TA in using reflection in her work.

Helping your TA become a reflective practitioner

As we have already stated, a good deal of attention has been paid to teacher reflection, but very little to TAs as reflective practitioners. However, the same concepts apply. Both the rationale for reflection and the methods that can be used will apply to your TA and her work.

Reflect and apply

Look back at the reflective activities that you listed in the earlier section of this chapter. Would those be appropriate activities for your TA? Does she already engage in them? Or would she need support to begin that process? Can you engage in any of those activities together as an instructional team? Make a note of some of your thoughts.

Jack Mezirow and other experts in reflective practice advocate collaboration.

In *Learning as Transformation* Mezirow states that:

> Learning theory must recognize the crucial role of supportive relationships and a supportive environment in making possible a more confident, assured sense of personal efficacy, of having a self more capable of becoming critically reflective of one's habitual and sometimes cherished assumptions and of having the self-confidence to take action on reflective insights.

This really emphasizes the need for collaboration between you and your TA in the reflective process. And of course it may not only be your TA whose confidence needs a boost and who needs a colleague to motivate her to engage in reflection and to then act on it. Even as the leader of the instructional team and the more highly qualified professional, you may find this process somewhat disconcerting. Alexis Walker, in a 1996 article discussing cooperative learning, recommends a teaching approach where the teacher has minimal power over pupils, but where – in an atmosphere of support – the pupils acquire their education by being involved as active partners in the process. Consider the points she makes in relation to this type of cooperative learning, and how they might apply to you and your TA learning together.

According to Alexis Walker, cooperative learning:

◆ recognizes that the learner has a role in helping to construct meaning
◆ views the teacher and the learner as collaborators in the learning process
◆ is based on the accepted truth that we learn more when we are actively engaged in the process
◆ gives the learner a stake in the outcome
◆ provides each person with an active role.

Walker also states that cooperative learning:

> ... changes pupils. It influences what they know and how they think about themselves and others. Furthermore, it recognizes them as unique individuals and respects them as learners and as knowers. (p. 328 of article)

This really is apt for you and your TA. Learning together, you can change, and part of that change is how you see yourself, in the sense that it can expand your horizons and expectations.

Reflect and apply

Think about some of the challenges you experience in the classroom. For example, think of a pupil who has annoying behaviour that you hope to change. Or think about how you can help your TA to work with a child whose behaviour is particularly difficult. Try to view this classroom difficulty as an opportunity to write your plan:

1) Describe the problem – what exactly is the child doing and under what circumstances is he or she doing it?
2) Decide why you think the child is behaving in that way.
3) Play the 'what if ... ?' game. The rules for this game are simple – there are none, and anything is possible – although it works much better if you play it with someone rather than alone. Take turns to ask the question, *what if ...* to propose possible causes or

→ *continued*

solutions to the problematic behaviour. For example, you may ask:

◆ What if he can't hear me when I ask him to do something?
◆ What if we could get him to write a book about himself and his behaviour?
◆ What if he really doesn't understand what we mean?

... and so on. Keep generating possibilities until you feel you have reached a point where you have at least expanded your thinking about the difficulty in question, and come closer to finding a possible solution that you can then test.

Metacognition

In the previous chapter we briefly discussed Social Constructivism, and looked at what this set of learning theories offers for how you can work with your TA as an adult learner. As a reminder, the four main principles of social constructivism are in the box below. In particular, the fourth principle, *metacognition*, or awareness of one's own learning, applies here when we discuss reflective practice. In Chapter 4 we listed two implications of this principle for what you do as the teacher and leader of the classroom team; that you help your TA to:

◆ understand that she is learning, and how she is learning
◆ appreciate the extent and limits of her knowledge and understanding so that she can acknowledge the gaps, and remain aware of the need for additional learning.

Although your TA is an adult, there is a great deal of transferability between the teaching you do with pupils and the teaching opportunities you can provide to your TA; between the learning theory that has been proposed for children, and the learning that adults experience. Let's look at each of these implications.

Principle 1: The learning process is one of interactions between the known and what is to be learned.

Principle 2: Learning is a social process, involving interaction with other people; this interaction allows for sharing of knowledge and understanding.

Principle 3: Learning is influenced by context, but may not transfer easily from one context to another.

Principle 4: Metacognition – awareness of one's own learning – is an important part of the learning process.

Reflect and apply

◆ What do you do to help your pupils realize that they are learning?
◆ How do you help them understand the process by which they are learning?
◆ How do you simultaneously instil in your pupils a sense that they are learning, but that there are limits to what they know and there is still much more to learn?
◆ How do you do each of these things for your TA?

_____

_____

_____

_____

If you are interested in understanding more about reflection, a particular source of information on reflective practice in the UK is the website of Reflective Learning-UK (details in the Appendix), which produces the journal *Reflective Practice*. Articles in the journal address different kinds of reflective practice, the way reflection can be most usefully taught and learned, and the links between reflection and the quality of the work carried out. This information is not restricted to the field of education. Reflective Learning-UK is, according to the website, 'dedicated to establishing and sustaining cultures for high individual performance, service improvement and workplace transformation through the principles and practices of appreciative reflection.'

Elizabeth Clayden and her colleagues, in a 1994 article discussing learning, talk about the need to recognize that learning takes place in a context, rather than in a vacuum. (This is similar to the discussion we referred to in the last chapter, where Jean Lave and Etienne Wenger talked about legitimate peripheral participation.) They cite Brown and colleagues' definition of learning as 'a process of enculturation', and point out how important it is for learning to be situated in the culture to which it applies. Culture, as it applies to the work you do with your TA, relates to:

◆ the culture of the school
◆ the culture of your classroom (that is, how you run your classroom)
◆ the culture of the learner (your TA).

Clayden and her colleagues also talk about the need for 'authentic' learning activities – that is, those which belong to and are part of the ordinary practices of the local (classroom) culture. This includes learning to use tools (the practices, concepts and procedures) that an experienced practitioner (in this case, the teacher) uses. If learning situations do not meet these criteria for authentic activities, it is unlikely that true learning will take place, because the learner will not necessarily be able to generalize or transfer knowledge from the theoretical or simulated learning situation to the setting where it is to be used. For your TA, an example of this might be giving her reading material from a textbook or notes from training that you have yourself attended and found useful. She may understand – in theory – what she is reading, but she will not necessarily be able to translate or transfer that theory into everyday practice and identify examples of it in your classroom.

Transfer – what Elizabeth Clayden and her colleagues call 'the capacity to use knowledge to learn' – is essential. Teaching and classroom knowledge, for example, is not just a well-defined and limited box of tricks or procedures (what they call 'inert knowledge') but is much more usefully the 'working practices of a domain or discipline' with learning as enculturation into these practices. These ideas will resurface in a later chapter on collaboration. But they are pertinent to this discussion because reflection is one of the means by which you can create authentic learning opportunities for your TA. As you engage in reflective discourse with your TA, you can make explicit the links and meaning of what your TA is seeing in the classroom. You can help her use the knowledge she gains to promote transformation – new insights, new confidence about herself as a learner.

Teachers are encouraged to use reflection to become more aware of what they do and why they do it. You know that awareness is the first step towards change. Critical reflection is a deeper, more serious reflection that brings goals for change. Jennifer Coots and Kristin Stout, in their 2007 book *Critical Reflections about Pupils with Special Needs,* talk about customizing knowledge through critical reflection, which involves a process of interpretation. They suggest that teachers must develop local meaning in order to change their practices to align them with what is described in the literature as effective teaching. According to Timothy Reagan and colleagues, in their book *Becoming a Reflective Educator: How to Build a Culture of Enquiry in the Schools* (details in the Appendix), the benefits of systematic critical reflection are:

◆ reflective practice helps free teachers from impulsive, routine behaviour
◆ it allows teachers to act with deliberation, in an intentional manner
◆ it distinguishes teachers as human beings through this hallmark of intelligent action.

Researchers have also noted the significance of the link between thinking (critical reflection) and performing (workplace application), within organizational change.

Chapter summary

In this chapter we have looked at some of the possibilities and rationale for reflective practice in the classroom – for you and your TA as individuals, but perhaps more importantly as a classroom team. We have made the distinction between *reflection* and *critical reflection* where the latter requires a questioning not just of what happened and why, but of the underlying assumptions and meaning we ascribe to what happens. Critical reflection is not an easy process, because so much of what we do is instinctive and based on deeply held, but rarely articulated, beliefs about the world in general and our own particular place in it. Critical reflection is not a topic that can be covered in one small chapter, and we would recommend that you check the Appendix for further sources of information if it is something you wish to pursue. However, reflection is a practice – a habit, if you will – that is accessible to all practitioners, and that offers many potential benefits for your work with your TA.

6 | Collaboration

This chapter addresses principles of effective collaboration, as they apply to the work you do with your TA. First we need to clarify what we mean by the term *collaboration*. We use it in its broadest sense of working together. It could be considered synonymous with *cooperation*, *interaction* or *partnering*. However, we see collaboration as suggesting a level of commitment to common goals and purposes, with cooperation having more of a sense of an ad hoc agreement to comply, or be amenable to someone else's purposes or plans. When we talk of collaboration between teachers and TAs we are talking about a true partnership – a classroom team. This may sound somewhat idealistic, but we must hope for the ideal even if realistically it may not be easy to achieve.

Reflect and apply

Take a moment to think about the various ways in which you collaborate as a normal part of your school day or week. Think about those with whom you collaborate and why? Are you obliged to collaborate, or do you choose to do it? Consider the purposes and the effectiveness of those collaborations by completing the following statements:

I collaborate with: _____

We collaborate in order to: _____

The benefits of working together are: _____

_____

→ *continued*

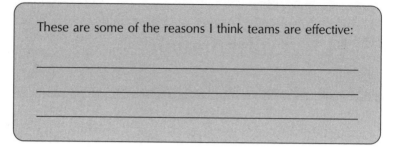

These are some of the reasons I think teams are effective:

Collaboration happens at many levels and for a variety of reasons within a school:

◆ Members of staff collaborate on organizational matters, coordinating timetables and physical arrangements (whether the hall or some item of audio-visual equipment is free at a particular time for an unscheduled activity; if they can swap a playtime supervision etc).

◆ Teachers collaborate on instructional matters, following curriculum guidelines to ensure that pupils have covered required material and developed expected skills before moving on to the next class, participating in INSET and staff meetings where specific curriculum areas are discussed in relation to the whole school, seeking and taking advice from a subject/curriculum coordinator etc.

◆ On a more general level, staff also cooperate with requests from the school's management team and secretarial staff to provide information, respond to parents, and allow for inevitable disruptions of the timetable (school photographer or nurse, artist in residence, students and trainees etc.).

◆ In the classroom as a teacher you ask pupils to collaborate: socially, to ensure that the classroom remains a pleasant and amenable learning environment, physically unthreatening and safe; on academic tasks in order to promote thinking and learning processes as pupils work on projects together.

◆ You may also ask pupils to cooperate with TAs and other adults who come to work in the classroom, as they deputize for you and work with individual pupils or small groups.

◆ Also in the classroom, you may work with a number of other adults – TAs of course, but also parent volunteers, peripatetic staff, student teachers etc. And of course this is the main focus of our discussions in this chapter.

Notice how often the prefix *co-* occurs in this discussion: *co*operate, *co*ordinate, *co*llaborate. It derives from the Latin word *cum* meaning *with* and, as is self-evident from this list, suggests working together with others. However, it is important to note here that for true collaboration to take place, *with* does not just mean *within the same physical space*, but must refer to deliberate and systematic working together for a common purpose with focus and efforts coordinated towards common goals. We do not feel the need to justify collaborative efforts between teachers and TAs. We assume that the fact that you are reading this book is evidence that you also see the need for true collaboration rather than just coexistence in the same physical space.

> Working together is more than occupying the same space – if it is to contribute to learning it must include working towards common goals.

The remainder of this chapter presents a variety of perspectives on collaboration, linking to the research as well as practical applications for the classroom.

You and your TA – the journey thus far

The first and most obvious collaboration in your classroom will be between you and your TA. We have already discussed many aspects of this version of collaboration. Indeed, the whole of the book so far has focused on the different ways in which you work with your TA:

♦ generally supervising the classroom team
♦ delegating responsibilities to your TA and making clear the roles you wish her to assume and those she does not need to feel responsible for
♦ ensuring accountability by monitoring the quality of her work, so that you can feel secure in her being an able deputy as she assists in the teaching and learning process in meaningful and effective ways; also for her own sense of achievement and satisfaction, in knowing that she is good at her work
♦ providing professional development through on-the-job training
♦ engaging in, and encouraging her to engage in, reflective practice, *and* engaging in reflection together through your focused

discussions and deliberate attempts at improving your effectiveness – as individuals and as a team

◆ and as we will discuss in the last chapter of the book, working together to find the time and resources to ensure the success of your joint endeavours.

These are all important aspects of classroom collaboration. In the Appendix you will find reference to a variety of resources specific to teachers and TAs working in collaboration, among them details of books by Glenys Fox and Maggie Balshaw, both produced by David Fulton Publishers, which offer very practical and focused advice for teachers and TAs.

TAs in collaboration – learning together

If you work with and supervise more than one TA, there are likely to be many occasions when you will ask them to work collaboratively, without your presence or intervention. What can you do to ensure that they work together in the most effective manner, and make optimal use of their efforts and strengths?

Sylvia McNamara and Gill Moreton, in their book *Understanding Differentiation*, devote a whole chapter to the importance of collaboration for learning. Their discussion focuses on pupils collaborating, but they make some useful points that apply here, particularly for two TAs working together:

◆ Being allowed to work collaboratively allows individuals to accomplish more than they could each accomplish alone.

◆ This contributes greatly to their self-esteem, as they can succeed in a paired or group effort where they might not be able to succeed – or succeed as fully – alone.

◆ The teacher can acknowledge and give credit for the collaborative efforts as much as for the content-related product of the collaboration, because collaboration does require effort and pupils should be rewarded for making that effort.

◆ Where there is a product, there should be evidence of both pupils having contributed to it, to ensure that one pupil did not do all the work while the other looked on. This is especially important where one of the partners is more assertive and confident, or more able, than the other.

Reflect and apply

With these recommendations, McNamara and Moreton are discussing collaboration among pupils. But take a moment to consider what application there may be for your TA. How do you see these principles translating into effective practice for TAs?

_____

_____

_____

_____

You might consider some of the following applications:

◆ If TAs are allowed to work together on appropriate tasks, they may well be able to accomplish more than they could by working alone, as each one contributes her own insights and skills to the task.

◆ Working together is likely to increase TAs' confidence in their own success, which in turn will contribute to increasing their self-esteem, as they see success from their joint effort.

◆ As the teacher you can indeed thank them for working well together to get the job done, in addition to acknowledging the product of their collaboration; this is something that you would want to encourage in your classroom, and certainly, when staff cannot work well together it is not only noticeable, it can have a detrimental effect on the atmosphere and productivity of the classroom.

Notice too that McNamara and Moreton are discussing collaboration _for learning_. This links back to previous discussions we have had about Social Constructivism:

◆ how meaning is derived from experience

◆ the importance of working with a more knowledgeable other (adult or peer), so that the learning process is scaffolded or supported

◆ the constructive discourse that Jack Mezirow states is critical for transformative learning.

All of these are inherent in collaborative endeavour, because it is unimaginable that two adults could work together in total silence, without exchanging views and building on each other's ideas, or observing each other's work and benefiting from it.

Interestingly, McNamara and Moreton begin their chapter on collaboration by discussing their own paired work as authors, and comment on the benefits they have found in working together on writing the book in question. They remark that the collaborative process is part of the enjoyment for them, and part of the learning that comes out of writing a book. We would certainly concur with these views. Through more than a decade of collaborating on a variety of writing projects, we have learned a great deal about ourselves and each other, our levels of skill (and tolerance!) as individuals, and the increased productivity that we can enjoy as we work together, rather than separately.

TAs who acquire HLTA status are also often required to supervise other TAs. This is considered acceptable under the Workforce Remodelling agreement. The HLTA handbook states that 'teaching and learning activities must take place under the direction and supervision of an assigned teacher and in accordance with arrangements made by the headteacher of the school'. However, HLTAs can work much more independently than TAs, and can participate in the full range of teaching activities undertaken by teachers.

> Those awarded HLTA status must demonstrate, through their practice, that they direct the work, where relevant, of other adults in supporting learning.
>
> *- Higher Level Teaching Assistant Candidate Handbook*

Standard 6 for HLTA status is: Demonstrate a commitment to collaborative and cooperative working with colleagues. As the *HLTA Candidate Handbook* states:

This standard is about demonstrating collaborative and cooperative working with a range of other adults according to the individual educational setting. It is about acknowledging the role of others as well as the scope and limitations of the role of teaching assistants in relation to other adults.

This standard acknowledges the need for collaborative efforts, even though those with HLTA status are permitted and expected to work with high levels of independence. This suggests that independence for the HLTA neither means solitude nor isolation from fellow educators. If you are responsible for a HLTA, you will need to add this level of collaborative work and training for her – continuing to work with her despite her more independent duties, as well as providing training for her in collaborative skills, at the very least by modelling those skills for her.

Apprenticeship – learning through working together

In Chapter 4 we referred to Jean Lave and Etienne Wenger's work on situated learning where *newcomers*, as they refer to them, gradually build their expertise by participating in the work situation alongside a master or expert. They refer to the newcomer's participation as legitimate, because they have every right to be there in that situation, but peripheral, because their limited skills and knowledge do not allow them to participate fully in all the functions of the master. This apprenticeship type of situation, where your TA is learning on-the-job, or *in situ*, is another form of collaboration.

An analogy

There is a common phrase that provides some useful insight into the role of the TA, and that we might explore for a moment. We say, in various versions: 'She can't hold a candle to [someone]', meaning that she is less skilled than the other person. But the idiom originates in the context of traditional apprenticeships from previous centuries. One of the apprentice's duties, especially early on in his training, would be to hold a light so that the Master could see to carry out his work. And, of course, that light would have been a candle – the candle referred to in the idiom. Comparing a TA to an apprentice holding the candle for the Master may seem to suggest that she is working at the very lowest level of usefulness, doing a job that could be performed by even the newest and least skilled apprentice. But consider the deeper implications:

◆ without the light (held by the apprentice), the Master could not see to do his work, so the task of holding the light may have been a simple one, but it was essential

◆ implied in the idiom is the idea too that the candle needed to be held in order to shed light where it was especially needful; a lamp or candle simply placed near the Master as he worked was not enough – the light needed to be directed to focus on the particular task the Master was engaged in, and he was not able to both carry out that task and direct the light alone

◆ as the apprentice held the light, he was able to watch the Master at work, and thereby he learned his trade over the hours spent alongside the Master as he displayed his craftsmanship; as the apprentice was required to hold the light so that it shone on the particular aspect of the Master's work currently being carried out, the apprentice's attention would be drawn to the details of that part of the work.

Seen in this light (if you will excuse the pun), this seems like a perfect metaphor for your relationship with your TA. Working alongside and observing you, she can learn the craft of teaching as you model various aspects of it. But in working alongside you, she can also help to 'shed light on' what you do, so that you also see your work more clearly, and are able to carry it out more precisely.

Reflect and apply

Stop and think for a moment how your TA might 'enlighten' you in your work. What is it about having a TA present in your classroom (or even working under your direction in another part of the school) that would help you to better 'see' what you are doing, and therefore work more effectively? And what is the light she holds? What might the candle represent in the modern classroom situation with teacher and TA, rather than apprentice and Master? Make a few notes, or map out your thoughts.

_____

_____

_____

Notice too, that in this comparison between the apprentice–master relationship and your TA–teacher relationship, you are the equivalent of the Master – which indeed you are, as you have been trained in the craft of teaching. Even if you have not been practising that craft for very long, you have received focused and specific training (over the course of several years) in the craft of teaching, and are thereby qualified to take the lead and show the way.

We could summarize the analogy of the apprentice holding the candle as three principles:

◆ the apprentice performed essential work
◆ the work performed by the apprentice was focused on a specific aspect of the Master's work
◆ the focused efforts of the apprentice simultaneously facilitated the Master's work and offered learning opportunities for the apprentice.

These three principles could be translated into questions that you can ask yourself about the work you and your TA do *in collaboration*:

◆ Is the work I give my TA essential to my work as a teacher and facilitator of learning – or is it just fill/busy work?
◆ Is my TA's work linked to very specific and focused aspects of my work as a teacher?
◆ Does my TA's work facilitate mine *and* offer opportunities for my TA to learn?

These are obviously questions that only you can answer for your own classroom, but – if you are brave – you might ask your TA for her opinion, especially about the first question.

The teamwork research

Another synonym for collaboration is *teamwork*. There is a large body of research into what constitutes an effective team, although relatively little of that research has been carried out in the field of education, and much of it is anecdotal. We have already referred to you several times in this book as the leader of the classroom or instructional team, and this is the level of teamwork we have focused on through the book and will focus on in this chapter. Thus, when we talk of collaboration or teamwork, we are looking at small teams (quite possibly just you and your TA) and would recommend that you focus your efforts to begin with on the smallest unit in which you and your TA are involved. If you have involvement on a wider level in the school (as part of a departmental or subject-based team in a secondary school, for example) you may find it helpful to consider some of the principles we have discussed in relation to the smallest unit first, and then move outward to the larger teamwork.

From the research into team effectiveness, a number of important points emerge:

◆ the need for a clear and united purpose, expressed in terms of team goals – which all team members are aware of and committed to
◆ the importance of each team member understanding his or her role in working towards those goals
◆ the need for clear and honest communication – including the time required to discuss planning and evaluate team progress
◆ the importance of sharing power among team members so that no individual feels disenfranchised.

The research also suggests that team members should receive training in how to be an effective team. In education this is extremely rare, and few teachers receive training in how to supervise TAs – either during their initial teacher training, or subsequently as a qualified practitioner. It is becoming more common now for teachers and their TAs to receive training together, in a subject area common to both of their roles, but this is most often likely to be true for those working in special needs settings, and does not usually include training in team skills. In mainstream classrooms where there is a TA, when the teacher is absent to attend training, the TA provides continuity for the class, and all too often is not therefore released to attend the training with her teacher.

Effective teams have:

◆ a clear and united purpose or set of goals, which all team members are committed to
◆ team members who understand their roles in working towards team goals
◆ clear and honest communication, with time allocated for planning and evaluating team progress
◆ shared power so that no individual feels disenfranchised.

Another interesting point from the teamwork research is the relative merits of diversity among team members in terms of skills and approaches to their work. Although it may be comfortable to work with people who see things the way you do, the research suggests that the teams most likely to be creative in problem-solving are those where there is diversity in approach and outlook. No doubt you have found that you and your TA can complement each other with your differing backgrounds, experience and skills. If you have had significant differences of outlook or approach to a TA, you may have felt the need to supervise more actively. But hopefully you have also been able to see the benefits of working with someone who sees things differently and can therefore help with problem-solving as well as being creative in different ways from your own.

Teamwork or co-teaching?

Of course, even your most focused and deliberate collaboration and working together with your TA is not necessarily synonymous with co-teaching or team teaching. In the 1960s and '70s, the idea of co-teaching was widely promoted in schools (in the UK and elsewhere). This movement fizzled out, however, partly because of a general reluctance on the part of teachers to teach with another qualified teacher present. The research suggests that teachers found it far too inhibiting and intimidating. However, this was not only a question of shyness or a fear of being judged inadequate. The time required for planning and coordination was also considered prohibitive, and the benefits were considered not worth the effort. Historically teachers have had a great deal of autonomy in their own classrooms, and as we have already said, even now they do not typically receive training in leading a classroom team. The idea of teaching in the presence of another adult – fellow teacher or TA – is still intimidating to many teachers, although with the increased numbers of TAs in UK schools, very few teachers now teach alone.

Sadly, the research also suggests that there is little benefit to pupils' achievement levels merely by having extra adults in the classroom. If the adults' efforts are not coordinated towards increasing pupil achievement, but are merely a division of labour ('*You read the story at the end of the afternoon while I finish preparing for the morning*'), then they will not affect pupil achievement in a positive way. Merely handing a child over to another adult will not necessarily help that child progress. The factors that will improve the likelihood of progress for the child include:

◆ the TA understanding the importance of the current activity to the needs of the child and in relation to the prescribed curriculum
◆ the TA having the skills necessary to help the child in the particular ways he or she needs help/support.

Reflect and apply

We discussed TA roles and the delegation of duties to your TA in Chapter 2. But think again about the tasks you assign your TA. Are they focused on pupil achievement? What is it about those tasks that will help a child progress and do better than he or she would without the TA? Are there other tasks you could assign to your TA that would be more focused on pupil achievement than what she currently does?

_____

_____

_____

_____

Whatever the tasks you assign your TA, we would remind you that you should be specific in your requests. Taking time to think about those assignments can help you analyse those that are effectively delegated. Of course, we want to look at all the classroom tasks we do in light of what leads to pupil achievement.

Meredith Belbin is an acknowledged expert on teamwork in the UK. Although he comes to it from a background in industry and business, the principles he espouses relate very well to education and classroom teams. In his book *Team Roles at Work*, Belbin states that, 'teamwork is one of the most efficient ways we know of accomplishing complex tasks'. Teaching is undeniably a complex task. But we may well ask what makes teamwork an efficient way of completing or carrying out that task. Using the analogy of team sports, Belbin suggests:

> A good team comprises players who restrict their activities so as to avoid diminishing the role of others but who play their own role with distinction.

What is noticeable about this, is that he makes no distinction between different members of the team – the team captain, for example, as opposed to other team members. The captain is presumably considered to be one of the players who should be restricting their own activities so as not to interfere with the other players in their assigned roles; and the captain must concentrate on playing his or her own role 'with distinction'. This suggests a very hands-off approach for the team leader or captain – a *stand back and let them get on with it* attitude that you may not be comfortable with, and that may seem to contradict some of what we have said in previous chapters about monitoring the work of your TA.

Teamwork – one of the most efficient ways we know of accomplishing complex tasks.

– Meredith Belbin

Reflect and apply

How would you reconcile the two apparently contradictory ideas of monitoring your TA's work, and – as Belbin has suggested – restricting your own activities 'so as to avoid diminishing' your TA in her role? Can these two ideas coexist?

_____

_____

_____

_____

We have seen many classrooms where teachers and TAs participate on an equal footing, and do whatever needs to be done to support learning. However, we have also seen too many classrooms where the lead teacher stands back to let the lowest paid do the 'dirty' work. When the team leader makes comments such as, 'I never do *that* type of work, that's her job', you are bound to encounter problems with that team. There is no doubt that the teacher holds the responsibility for curricular decisions etc., but diminishing the TA to a 'lesser role' (and pointing it out to everyone) does not help the sense of cameraderie and respect that promotes effective teamwork. The idea of 'serving with distinction', as a team player, a teacher, or a school unit sits well with the concepts of effective collaboration. And if you think back to Chapter 4, we referred you to Lave and Wenger's idea of legitimate peripheral participation. You may recall that we included their caveat that the apprentice can be disempowered if the Master limits the apprentice's participation unnecessarily. There is a fine balance between involving and trusting your TA fully as a team member whose skills are valued, and ensuring quality control by setting certain limits on your TA's role and level of autonomy.

Meredith Belbin also suggests that the ability to work as a team member may be more important than the precise skills that an individual brings to the team. This makes sense if you consider that a good team member must be willing to learn and contribute appropriately to the team; what he or she lacks in skills can then be acquired through the collaborative team process.

Another author of interest is Ken Blanchard with his book *Gung Ho* (which purportedly means 'working together' in Chinese). In this book, Blanchard puts forward three principles, or guideposts, based on native American Indian wisdom:

Guidepost 1: The spirit of the squirrel – worthwhile work
Guidepost 2: The way of the beaver – in control of achieving the goal
Guidepost 3: The gift of the goose – cheering each other on

The details of these guideposts are listed in the box.

Three guideposts or principles proposed by Ken Blanchard in his book *Gung Ho*:

Guidepost 1: The spirit of the squirrel - worthwhile work

◆ knowing we make the world better
◆ working towards a shared goal
◆ plans, decisions and actions are guided by values.

Guidepost 2: The way of the beaver - in control of achieving the goal

◆ clearly marked territory
◆ everyone's thoughts, feelings and needs listened to and acted on
◆ tasks that are challenging but possible.

Guidepost 3: The gift of the goose - cheering each other on

◆ *true* acknowledgement of accomplishments (timely, responsive, unconditional, enthusiastic)
◆ no keeping score - it's not a game - but acknowledgement of progress made
◆ E = mc2 (enthusiasm = mission x (cash and congratulations)).

Reflect and apply

Take a moment to read the details of Blanchard's guide-posts, and consider how they could apply to your work with your TA. Jot down your reactions to the following questions:

◆ Does my TA know that her work makes a difference? (How does she know that? How do I communicate it to her?)

◆ Are my TA and I working towards a shared goal, or set of goals? (What are those goals? How were they decided? How have I communicated them to her?)

◆ What is the basis for our plans, decisions and actions? Is our work driven by targets imposed by agencies outside the classroom, or by the values we share and acknowledge in our work?

◆ Do each of us have clearly marked 'territory' and responsibilities?

◆ Do I listen to – and act upon – my TA's thinking, feelings and needs?

◆ Do I give my TA tasks that are challenging but realistic?

◆ Do I acknowledge my TA's accomplishments in a timely and responsive fashion, showing unconditional enthusiasm?

◆ Do I acknowledge progress, not just finished products?

_____

_____

_____

_____

This is obviously more than you can answer in a short space of time, and indeed several of these questions relate back to previous chapters and discussions in this book. You will need time to address and answer each one; and as things change in the supervision you provide for your TA, they will most certainly need to be revisited.

And lastly, as an additional perspective that may help to focus your thinking about teamwork and collaborative effort, we mention Peter Senge, author of *The Fifth Discipline*, a book in which he discusses what he calls *learning organizations*. Although his discussion is focused primarily on business organizations, he makes the point early on that these principles have much broader application, including schools and families. The four main disciplines for learning organizations he lists as being:

◆ *Personal mastery*, in terms of seeking to become a master of whatever craft you are practising, and actively pursuing personal growth.

◆ *Mental models* – here Senge is referring to the basic assumptions underlying our decisions and outlook, which we referred to in Chapter 5 when we discussed the importance of *critical* reflection.

◆ *Building shared vision*, as opposed to just sharing your vision with those who work with you.

◆ *Team learning*, which Senge insists must include dialogue – a free flow of ideas through a willingness to think together rather than defending one's own ideas.

The fifth discipline of the book title is *systems thinking* – trying to see the bigger picture rather than only focusing on tackling small, individual difficulties that are often caused by larger systematic flaws. This is obviously no easy matter, and Senge has dedicated over 400 pages to it, but we include it (and recommend the book as an interesting read) because of the commonalities with the other perspectives we have discussed in this chapter.

Reflect and apply

In light of the information we have provided from Senge's 'bigger picture' of collaboration, and your earlier reading on Belbin's and Blanchard's concepts, which of these do you relate to your collaborative teamwork? Use the perspectives from this chapter to guide your thinking as you create a plan for building a collaborative classroom culture. What activities could serve as a catalyst for building collaboration?

_____

_____

As you reflect on the collaboration in your classroom, this may be a good time to meet with your team to review what you do well, and celebrate achievements. It could also be a good time to reflect on additional goals your team can set towards improving collaboration within the classroom or on a school level.

Chapter summary

In this chapter we have looked at collaboration from a number of different perspectives:

♦ The activities that you and your TA engage in together, and that have formed the subject of the previous chapters in this book.

♦ The collaborations that so often occur between TAs, where we presented some of the ideas of Sylvia McNamara and Gill Moreton about how to use collaboration to induce and enhance learning opportunities; while McNamara and Moreton were discussing collaborations between pupils, the principles transfer well to a situation where two TAs are working together and can learn from that experience, particularly if that collaboration includes the type of 'constructive discourse' recommended by Jack Mezirow.

♦ Jean Lave and Etienne Wenger's work on situated learning with its emphasis on apprenticeship and how this relates to collaboration between you and your TA – again with the purpose of teaching the TA or allowing her opportunities to learn from your expertise.

♦ The research on what constitutes effective teamwork, including Meredith Belbin's view of teamwork as the most efficient means of 'accomplishing complex tasks'.

♦ Ken Blanchard's view of working together, which draws on native American wisdom.

♦ Peter Senge's five disciplines of the learning organization – which, as a classroom team, teachers and TAs surely are.

We have presented this variety of perspectives on collaboration and teamwork because we feel that they have much to offer in terms of provoking thinking and discussion about how collaboration works. Some of the perspectives will appeal to you more than others; one in particular may suggest more meaningful applications to your work than the others. They all have something to offer. Use whichever you find most useful.

7 | Logistics

In this chapter we consider some of the practicalities of supervising TAs – how supervision works in the day-to-day bustle of classrooms, and how you can overcome some of the apparently natural barriers to establishing and maintaining an effective classroom team. In particular we will look at:

◆ time – time to meet together and plan your work – how that can be found in a busy day and on a regular basis
◆ evaluation or assessment of your TA – how that can fit in with the activities you both engage in
◆ advocating for your TA – the many ways in which you can mediate and facilitate opportunities for your TA, both within the school and outside.

John Sosik and Veronica Godshalk, two American authors discussing leadership skills in 2000, talk about the 'psychosocial support' leaders give to those under their jurisdiction. In particular they mention a variety of 'career development' functions of an effective leader, including:

◆ sponsorship
◆ protection
◆ exposure
◆ visibility.

They advocate providing this type of psychosocial support, as well as tangible resources, as a means of empowering others and making their efforts more effective. TAs have historically been a disempowered group with no formal representation or organization to advocate for their needs. Their value has been appreciated by those who work most closely with them – teachers, pupils and parents. However, they have not been formally recognized in the ways society accepts as denoting importance – proper pay structures and career paths, the sense of being engaged in a profession, being fully included in the organization where they work, belonging to professional organizations. Only recently, since government legislation with the Workforce Remodelling Initiative, has their role in the organizational infrastructure of the education system been recognized, valued, and somewhat formalized.

'Career development' functions of an effective leader:

◆ sponsorship
◆ protection
◆ exposure
◆ visibility

John Sosik and Veronica Godshalk, 2000

Reflect and apply

Think about those terms that Sosik and Godshalk proposed – *sponsorship, protection, exposure, visibility* and *tangible resources* – in relation to your TA. How can (or do) you sponsor and protect your TA? Under what circumstances would she need your sponsorship? Why would she need protecting? From whom or what? And what should you expose her to? Why should she become more visible? What tangible resources should you provide her with?

That is a long list of questions, but we will try to answer them (or help you answer them for your own situation and your TA) in the rest of the chapter.

Time

The first question that usually comes to mind when teachers think of supervising TAs is, *Where will we find the time?* This is a real concern, because supervision (as all you have read in this book so far attests) encompasses a wide range of activities for the supervising teacher.

◆ TAs need to know their role ... but someone has to take the time to provide that information (even if it is handed over in written form, it takes time to consider and write).
◆ TAs need to know what is expected of them on a day-to-day basis, as needs change and plans are adapted as part of the regular dynamics of schools ... and someone needs to take the time to inform them.

And so on, through planning for student needs and collaborative efforts, giving and receiving feedback on activities and students etc. Supervision takes time. That has to be accepted as a reality and it will require considerable ingenuity on your part if you are committed to providing systematic supervision for your TA.

Supervision takes time!

It may be useful here to consider the basis on which you are taking decisions about what you can do to better supervise your TA.

Reflect and apply

Which of these two statements best describes your attitude and approach to supervision?

◆ I would prefer it if my TA and I could get together and plan our work.
◆ As a matter of principle, I believe teachers and TAs should be able to get together and plan their work.

When we express ourselves in terms of *preferences* there is usually a good deal of room for negotiation. We would prefer one thing, but:

◆ we recognize that other people's preferences may be different
◆ we are willing to compromise and meet others halfway
◆ unless their preferences go against our principles we may be willing to cede entirely to their preferences on this occasion
◆ we readily see obstacles in our way that would seem to prevent us from doing what we would prefer.

On the other hand, when we talk in terms of *principles*, there is usually very little room for negotiation:

◆ this is a question of our basic assumptions of the rules or moral and ethical standpoints we use to govern our lives
◆ we feel justified in standing our ground and insisting, even in the face of stiff opposition.

So when we talk of finding time to collaborate and plan with your TA, if this is a question of *principle* for you, the chances are that you will find the time, no matter how difficult it may be. If it is only a matter of *preference*, then other priorities (principles) will most likely take up the time that could be given to actively supervising your TA. We would hope that the management team in your school would recognize the importance of allocating space on your timetable, but this is often difficult logistically, with all the demands made on the timetable, and they may not yet be 'converted' to the idea. In addition, when TAs are assigned to work for a designated number of hours per week with a particular child, Heads may feel that they cannot take any of those hours away for what they consider administrative − rather than educational − tasks. Whether any of this is 'right', it certainly is likely to be the practical reality you face as a supervisor.

It is also worth considering that time for supervision comes into several categories, as we have already stated:

◆ time to plan
◆ time to actively collaborate
◆ time for monitoring your TA's work
◆ time to provide feedback and discuss progress.

These are all areas of supervision that require your time. What you have to decide is how often you need to spend time on each of these areas, how much time, and − the real crux of the matter − where you will find the necessary time. This is very much a matter of personal preference, moderated by the other demands on your time as a teacher, but here are some thoughts that may help you in taking decisions:

◆ Activities such as planning are part of what you do in the course of your teaching, whether you have a TA or not. Long-term planning is obviously carried out less frequently than medium- or short-term planning. This will also be true of the planning you do with your TA. When you involve her in the planning process, the relative amounts of time she needs to be involved will vary according to the type of planning you are doing.

◆ Some of the planning you do is out of your control – the content dictated by the National Curriculum, for example, or the guidelines of the Foundation Phase in Wales – so you may not feel it necessary to include your TA in the long-term planning at all, even though she needs to be familiar with the framework within which you are both working. You may even feel this way about medium-term planning. But your TA will have valuable insights to add to the short-term planning you do, and this would be the level at which you definitely need to spend time planning together.

◆ Consider the principle of immediacy. Weigh up the relative merits of written versus spoken communication with your TA. There will be some types of information you need from her, or she needs from you, which can very usefully be written down because they are not critical in terms of time. You can read the notes she has written about a particular activity with an individual child at your leisure. Although this reading takes time, it can be done at your convenience. (An added benefit of writing notes for your TA is that she must reflect on the activity in order to write notes, and will hopefully gain insight by doing it. But don't forget to allow her time to write the notes during her working hours!) Likewise if you have information for her – on a course you have attended or something you would like her to do that is not urgent – you can give them to her in written form, rather than having to find a time that is mutually convenient to pass the information on, and she can read them at her leisure. These written communications can supplement your face-to-face meetings and discussions.

◆ Monitoring your TA's work (which we discussed in a previous chapter on accountability) is most effectively done in small time slots. If you give all of your attention to it, you can gain a great deal of useful information about her effectiveness in just 10–15 minutes. You do not have to spend hours watching her work.

Better to set aside your other responsibilities, and spend less time observing closely and making notes, than trying to keep an eye on her for longer periods of time while engaged in your other responsibilities.

◆ How often you monitor your TA's work is partly determined by the types of tasks she is assigned and her level of skill in those tasks. If you know she is competent in a particular area of her work, you obviously only need to check occasionally that things are going as smoothly as you hope. When you ask her to take on new tasks – or ones for which you are unsure of her level of skill – you obviously need to check more often, until you are confident of her competence. There is a simple logic to this, but also a simple conclusion: do not assign your TA too many tasks for which you are unsure of her competence; gradually introduce new areas of work. This not only makes fewer demands on your time in monitoring her work, but also ensures that she is working effectively as your deputy, in areas where she is competent.

◆ When you do meet to give feedback or discuss a particular child's progress and needs, you can set a time limit for the meeting. Short, frequent meetings are most likely to be efficient, and if you meet on a sufficiently regular basis, you should be able to cover what you need to in each meeting. Karen Vincett and her colleagues recommend 15 minutes for what they call 'planning' meetings – that is, the meetings where teacher and TA discuss the strengths and weaknesses of a particular teaching session. The teachers and TAs in their study held these planning meetings daily.

These sorts of activities would all come under the heading of protection: protecting the quality of the education your pupils receive; protecting your TA from working in situations where she feels uninformed and lacking in confidence; and protecting the integrity of your work as you enable your TA to deputize effectively for you.

You know your own class routine best, so we would not presume to advise you as to where the time will come from to supervise your TA. In the same way that you find time for other activities that you feel are important – by setting your pupils tasks that they can confidently complete independently, for example – so you will be able to find time to supervise, if that is a priority for you.

Useful principles for identifying time to supervise your TA

◆ An activity such as planning is part of what you do as a teacher. When you involve your TA in planning, the amount of time will vary according to the type of planning you are doing.

◆ You may not feel it necessary to include your TA in long-term or medium-term planning, but she will have valuable insights to add to short-term planning.

◆ Weigh up the relative merits of written versus spoken communication. Various forms of written communications can supplement your face-to-face meetings and discussions.

◆ Monitoring your TA's work is most effectively done in small time slots. Set aside time for observing her closely and making notes, rather than trying to keep an eye on her while you do your other work.

◆ How often you monitor your TA's work partly depends on her level of competency in tasks she is assigned. The closest monitoring is needed when you assign new tasks, or ones for which you are unsure of her level of skill.

◆ When you do meet, set a time limit for the meeting. Short, frequent meetings are most efficient.

Evaluation

We have already dedicated a whole chapter to this area of your supervisory responsibilities, but we refer to it again here because this is an area where you can advocate for your TA, particularly with the Head and the school management team. Take, for example, the annual appraisal process. For those TAs who have an appraisal (and many still do not) this is most often carried out by the Head or another senior member of staff, rather than the TA's immediate supervisor. And the most common form of appraisal is a one-off observation. However, such an observation is a very detached form of evaluation, and only provides a snapshot of the TA's work (and under the pressure of being observed by a senior member of staff!). Whenever possible, such a snapshot should be supplemented by more general comments on the TA's work by the person who works most closely with her. And if the

TA is to be observed, it is always helpful for the observer to understand the context of her work before the observation – what her assigned task is, the limitations of the work you have asked her to do, the particular areas you may be working on together – or the skills that she is working on improving. This then is another area in which you can protect your TA – in this instance, from potential unnecessary and unfair criticism by providing a context for any evaluation carried out by someone who may not be well informed about her work.

Advocating for your TA

This is an area in which Sosik and Godshalk's list of career development functions – sponsorship, protection, exposure, and visibility – provided as psychosocial support by a leader, especially come into play. As the person who works most closely with a TA, you are the person who is most conversant with her strengths and needs, and are her natural advocate and sponsor. Past experience has shown that there are three main areas in which teachers may need to advocate for their TAs. These include:

◆ Continuing Professional Development
◆ providing references or other forms of recommendation
◆ the TA's status and standing in the school

We will consider each of these separately.

Continuing Professional Development

We have already dedicated a whole chapter to discussing ways in which you can provide CPD for your TA in terms of on-the-job training and in collaboration with other staff at the school. However, there will be aspects of her job for which it would be helpful for her to have CPD outside of the school environment. The type of intensive training provided by the LEA, where a topic is covered over the course of a day, or even two, can be so very useful because it typically provides an overview of principles and theory, as well as some practical application. On completion of the training, your TA can report back to you, and together you can discuss how the training relates to her specific work responsibilities in your classroom. The major obstacle to sending TAs to outside training is generally funding, as there may be no dedicated funding for TA training – either in the school budget or from outside sources. This is a difficult issue for your TA to address with the Head or other senior management person (particularly in a large secondary school), but it is an area in which you can offer sponsorship and advocacy. If you request such funding as her supervising teacher, you add weight to the application as you confirm the necessity of the training to her current work in your classroom, or to roles that you would like to assign her but for which you feel she needs more training.

You can find out more about available government funding for TAs to access training on the DCFS Standards site (details in the Appendix). In particular, 'Skills4schools' has been developed by UNISON, Britain's largest trade union (which has more than 1.3 million members, a growing number of whom are TAs). Also, Open College is what UNISON terms its 'flexible learning arm', designed to encourage and promote members' career development. Again, the details of how you can access this information are in the Appendix.

These are some other potential funding sources:

◆ your LEA may have monies set aside for training TAs
◆ some of the professional associations such as the Association of Teachers and Lecturers offer training for TAs who are members and/or funds for them to attend other training
◆ if your TA wishes to enrol on a formal course of study, there are often means-tested bursaries or grants available, which the institution of further or higher education would be able to advise on.

Providing references and other types of recommendation

Although you would not wish to lose your TA – particularly once you have developed a strong working relationship with her and provided her with opportunities for CPD to enhance her skills and knowledge – she may wish to take up other employment opportunities as they arise. This will be increasingly likely as government guidelines establish career pathways for TAs and a wider variety of opportunities for 'promotion'. But she may also ask you to support an application for voluntary work or after-school opportunities. As the person who has worked most closely with her, monitored her skills and worked with her on areas for improvement and professional development, you are well placed to comment on her abilities and to provide her with the sort of references that can be very specific and directly related to her work as a TA.

In a previous chapter on CPD, we also recommended that you work with your TA to develop a portfolio demonstrating her experience, skills and knowledge. TAs who wish to achieve HLTA status, must develop a portfolio documenting the ways in which they have demonstrated competency in relation to the HLTA standards. (And just another reminder that HLTA is a status, not a qualification. The training provided for aspiring HLTAs covers how to gather and present evidence of competency, rather than teaching the underlying principles of effective practice that would enable TAs to meet the standards.) The format of the HLTA portfolio is very specific. But the model is useful to this discussion in that it requires a TA to build a portfolio that evidences her skills and experience. This is a useful way for any TA to provide evidence of skills and knowledge, as well as professional development undertaken, either formally through a course offered outside school, or informally through on-the-job training that you provide. The box lists items that could be included in a portfolio. In addition to demonstrating the TA's skills, knowledge and qualifications, the portfolio can serve other purposes:

◆ to support the TA's application for a higher level TA position in the current school, or as a general job application elsewhere
◆ to evidence an ethos of inclusion in the school
◆ as evidence of your competence as a supervisor
◆ appropriate to our discussion here, it would provide you with a detailed overview of your TA's skills and knowledge, as well as a reminder of the different training opportunities she has taken.

Why utilize a portfolio?

Documentation of evidence can show that the TA has the skills required for employment, as well as showing the development of skills to meet the new standards established for them. A popular way to organize the documentation is a portfolio. Portfolios have often been used in teacher training and are a natural extension for TAs. Portfolios can be a way for TAs to gather and show evidence that they have met the standards established. However, some types of material or evidence are more appropriate to include in a TA portfolio than others. Some types of material would be considered superfluous, because they give the portfolio more of the look of a scrapbook or personal memory book. Teachers can provide mentoring that will help TAs in their selection of appropriate materials. Portfolios can be used to spotlight existing experience. They can also encourage reflective practice.

There are two main types of portfolios: working and presentation.

◆ *The Working Portfolio* is a collection of evidences and reflections that demonstrate individual growth over time. These are guided by the standards of the TAs organization, and the programme learning objectives. They are generally quite large and will contain the information from which the TA will draw the Presentation Portfolio.

◆ *The Presentation Portfolio* is a public or semi-public demonstration of the TA's highest level of achievement through representative evidences and reflections.

So how do you know what types of evidence to collect? Use the analogy of a detective. What evidence does a detective consider in an investigation? It must be physical evidence. It may be the testimony of eye-witnesses, but not hearsay or second-hand provided by someone who heard it from someone else who perhaps saw the event.

The evidence of a TA's skills should be concrete, physical evidence. As the supervising teacher, you could include letters or other evidence of your 'eye-witness' accounts that the TA has met certain standards. Your letters or observations should be specific − they should say exactly what you observed and if and how it impacted pupils.

Lines of evidence
Some of the appropriate materials that could be included as lines of evidence are listed in the textbox.

Useful types of material to include in a portfolio

◆ performance evaluations
◆ evidence of in-service training observations and summaries of CPD opportunities
◆ coursework/certificates of completion
◆ written documents, such as letters of recommendation
◆ work samples, including photographs of projects undertaken
◆ videos of work performance
◆ letters of reference
◆ interview summaries or documents, and
◆ reflections on work and learning

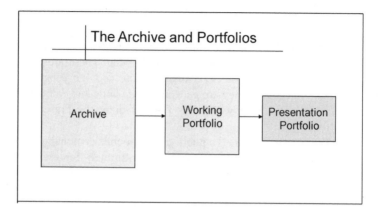

The materials included in the portfolio must be such that they will be considered evidence. Most of the items listed in the box clearly document evidence of professional development, training, and work related successes. However, it would be useful to say a little more about the last item – reflection.

Reflection
We have already discussed reflection in Chapter 5, but there we said little about documenting reflection. Reflection on practice fosters greater understanding of the processes at work in the classroom and helps in making wise and principled decisions. But reflection is also partly about self-knowledge – not only the ability to 'see through' teaching situations and understand the meaning of what is happening in the classroom, but also to see one's self and the effects of oneself as the teacher (or TA) within the situation. We have already said that critical reflection is a complex process. Tony and Kay Ghaye say that critical reflection should not just be a private, self-indulgent 'navel-gazing'. Nor should it be a process of self-victimization. Rather it should be about taking a questioning stance towards what teachers/TAs and schools do. Reflective practitioners are professional practitioners who understand their influence and its boundaries.

We have also referred to the importance of reflective discourse or conversation as being central to effective reflective practice. But one step further than this is to record your reflections in writing, which also helps to crystallize thinking and clarify dilemmas. You can prompt this written reflection by asking your TA to consider certain questions and record her thoughts. You can model the process by keeping a reflective journal of your own and referring to it when discussing classroom issues with your TA. And of course, in the absence of a colleague with whom to engage in reflective discourse, written reflection helps to keep reflections focused, as well as providing a written record that you can refer back to as needed.

Your TA's status and standing in the school

The third way in which you can advocate for your TA is to take steps to consider and enhance her status. This applies on two levels – your classroom and pupils, and with the rest of the school, that is, with other members of staff, including the Headteacher (or if you work at secondary level, the appropriate member of the school management team).

Reflect and apply

Take a moment to think about your TA's status in your classroom. This is not an easy exercise, because so much of what we do and communicate to others is subtle and subconscious. But ask yourself these questions:

◆ How do you have your pupils address your TA – by her first name, or as Miss/Mrs?

◆ How much autonomy and decision-making power do you allow her? Do your pupils see that she is allowed to take the initiative, or do they see that she always has to ask your permission or wait for your instructions?

◆ Do you uphold her decisions in public – especially those that relate to behaviour management? Or do pupils know that they can take liberties with her because she essentially has no clout?

Although you may have very good reasons for each of these aspects of her work, you should ask yourself whether this has a negative effect on pupils' perceptions of your TA as someone with less authority, lower skills and knowledge. *But these are all true!* we hear you protest – *she does have less authority and lower skills.* It may be true that she has fewer qualifications and less theoretical knowledge, and it is certainly true that you have more authority and responsibility for the classroom where you both work. However, she stands in for you, and that being the case, she needs to have status as an adult who is part of the teaching team. In Chapter 2 we looked at the roles you delegate to your TA. One of the things you delegate to her is authority – the authority to act in your name, as it were, because she assists you in accomplishing the work of the classroom. Although every adult who works in the school must establish their own authority to a certain extent – and this is certainly true at secondary level where there is a much more extensive hierarchy – as a teacher you can easily undermine, or just as easily help to establish, your TA's authority for your pupils.

In terms of the larger context of the school, not all teachers have direct responsibility for TAs, and among those who do, not all will view TAs in the same positive light you do. There are still many staffrooms in the UK where TAs are not welcome or where they sit at opposite ends of the room to the teaching staff; staff meetings to which TAs are not invited; schools where TAs may be outwardly praised and apparently valued but where there is still a sense of 'them and us', teachers and non-teachers. If that is true in your school you have a great deal of work to do in promoting your TA's status and standing in the school, in terms of sponsorship and protection, as well as exposure and visibility.

A teacher's attitude towards a TA, although it may be subtle, does communicate to the pupils. So first you need to be sure that you clearly communicate to your pupils (and others in the school) that your TA is your deputy and is authorized to speak on your behalf. Even in your own classroom, the status you assign to your TA, your actions, language and public attitude towards her and her work will affect the degree to which your pupils show respect for your TA and consider her a person with proper authority in the classroom.

Remember that authority lies in assigned status – as a teacher, you are recognized as a person with authority in the school – but it also lies in expertise. Your pupils respect you for your knowledge as much as for your official position. If you openly recognize and acknowledge your TA's expertise, that will also add to her stature in the classroom and the respect she is likely to be given by pupils.

If you feel it is appropriate, request that TAs be included in staff meetings and trainings. If the school has a policy of only inviting teachers to staff meetings, and does not consider that TAs need to be there, look out for particular staff meetings or training sessions that would be especially appropriate for TAs, and request that they be involved as an exception to the general rule on those occasions. When information is being given out to staff, make a point of asking for a copy for your TA (or letting the Head know that you would like to make a copy for your TA and asking for permission to do so). Whenever the Head or governors are asking for feedback from teaching staff on some aspect of school life, make a point of asking whether you should also ask for your TA's opinion or feedback – and then make sure you ask her to participate in the feedback process. Whenever it seems appropriate, seek clarification about the role and responsibilities of TAs if a new procedure is discussed in staff meetings or being implemented. And the converse of that would be to question occasions when responsibilities are assigned to TAs that you feel they are unprepared for, or for which they need particular training.

At the risk of becoming very predictable with your new mantra of, 'And what about our TAs?', if you sincerely believe that your TA is making a valuable contribution to the learning process, you may need to be the school's conscience, as it were, in making sure that that contribution is not forgotten or underplayed.

Chapter summary

In this chapter we have been considering some of the logistics of supervision, and how it can work in with your other (many!) responsibilities as a teacher. We have framed this discussion in terms suggested by John Sosik and Veronica Godshalk when they suggest that effective leaders offer a range of career development supports to those they are responsible for: that is, sponsorship, protection, exposure, and visibility. Under these headings we have looked at the importance of:

◆ determining and finding the time necessary to collaborate effectively with your TA
◆ ensuring that evaluations carried out by senior members of staff are given a proper context
◆ advocating CPD opportunities for your TA, especially those that are provided outside school and for which funding may be needed
◆ providing references or other forms of recommendation for which you are most well placed as her supervisor
◆ advocating for your TA in terms of her status or standing in the school and in your classroom.

These are all part of the nuts and bolts of supervision, and we recognize that they are all additional to your basic responsibilities as a teacher and instructional leader. But they are all important aspects of effective supervision of your TA, as they establish her credibility and authority within the school, and serve to highlight the many valuable contributions she makes to the success of the school's endeavours.

Conclusions

We hope that this book has provided you with useful information for carrying out your role of supervisor of a TA. In conclusion, we would like to review the areas we have covered, and draw the different strands or elements together to see how they fit and work with each other.

In Chapter 1 (Supervising the Classroom Team) we looked at:

- Who you are responsible for as a supervisor. This question is very clear-cut if your TA works only with you or works with you for specified time slots during the week – the most common situation in primary settings. It becomes more complicated when TAs are assigned to specific children and move around the school with them, as is common in secondary schools.
- What supervision is – how you would define it, and the various official definitions available to us. Here we also looked at some of the purposes of supervision, particularly its potential in raising standards and pupil achievement – a point that obviously links to Chapter 3 (Accountability).
- What the government and legal guidelines or framework are for supervising TAs. The most prominent government document relating to TAs in recent years has been the National Agreement for workforce remodelling, which, in redefining teachers' roles, has also redefined the role of the TA.

We also referred to some of the recent research in the UK relating to teachers and TAs working together, and asked you to consider your own preferred supervision style – are you laid-back about it or a more hands-on supervisor? Whichever style you naturally (or deliberately) adopt, it will be a lens through which you view your responsibilities and the advice we have provided. It will also determine the extent to which you engage in supervision activities such as those we have recommended. We have referred constantly in this book to *your TA* – this has been deliberate, because we hope there is a sense of ownership about the supervision process.

In Chapter 2 (Delegating Responsibilities) we looked at aspects of your responsibilities as a teacher that can be delegated to your TA – within the law, within reason, according to your preferences and those of your TA, and according to the stated purposes of school and education. We considered the need for detailed job descriptions for TAs – not only of the generic sort used by the LEA or school for job applications, but specific to your TA and your classroom – which means specific to the needs of your pupils. As part of this definition process, we strongly recommended that you define the limits of your TA's role for her – elements that are *not* her responsibility as well as those that are. We also asked you to consider your TA's skills and training, so that you can be sure that she is competent for the tasks you delegate to her – or to look at the other side of the coin, that you do not delegate roles for which she is obviously lacking in the necessary skills or knowledge.

We acknowledge that your TA is an adult, and capable of letting you know if there are assignments for which she feels under-qualified, but as her supervisor, you do have to take the lead in determining her suitability for particular tasks – the extent to which you feel she can carry them out competently, despite lacking in confidence, and those she may be willing to take on, but that you really cannot justify assigning to her because she needs further training in those areas.

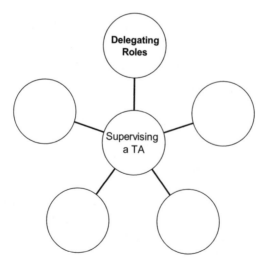

Chapter 3 (Accountability) was a discussion of the necessity of monitoring the quality of your TA's work, because she stands in for you and shares the task of promoting learning. You and she are accountable to several different groups of people – pupils, parents, the Head and school governors etc. There are also several important reasons for monitoring quality of work. We asked you to consider how and why you monitor your pupils' work, and whether those purposes and means of monitoring could be applied to your TA's work. Then we discussed the need for standards or benchmarks for performance and cited the NOS for TAs – now known as the Standards for Teaching and Learning in School – as well as the standards set for HLTA status. The last part of the chapter offered guidance on setting goals for improvement, using the SMART goal model.

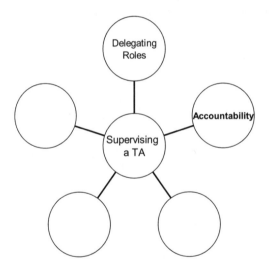

And of course this book is essentially about your accountability as a supervisor – particularly your accountability to your TA, but also as part of your larger responsibilities to your pupils as their teacher. You may not have asked for a TA – or perhaps you begged your Head to assign one to you. You may have felt that your TA was thrust upon you – or you may have done whatever was necessary to ensure that she was assigned to your classroom. You may prefer to work alone – or you may be most comfortable working as part of a team. Whichever the case, hopefully you value your TA's contributions. The fact that you are reading this book suggests that you want to maximize the value of those contributions and take your supervisory responsibilities seriously.

Chapter 4 (Providing Continuing Professional Development). We began this chapter by offering a variety of definitions of CPD, including the GTCW's statement that it 'encompasses all formal and informal learning which enables teachers to improve their own practice'. That very comprehensive definition suggests that there are many small ways in which you can offer development opportunities to your TA, and certainly that you do not have to rely on outside sources of training. Being responsible for another adult's learning has both similarities with, and differences from, being responsible for children and their learning. Your TA is an adult learner, which brings with it a whole set of possible uncertainties and insecurities, but many of the principles of learning apply equally well to adults and children. Many of the principles of teaching apply equally well to teaching children as teaching adults.

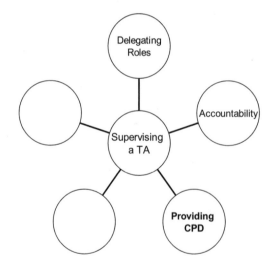

We referred you to the basic principles of Social Constructivism, including the views of experts such as Piaget, Vygotsky and Bruner. From this perspective, learning is a series of interactions between the known and the unknown, but happens most effectively as a social process, which allows for sharing of knowledge and understanding. Metacognition, or awareness of one's own learning, is also an important part of the learning process. The remainder of the chapter looked at some of the ways in which you can make professional resources available to your TA.

In Chapter 5 (Reflective Practice) we talked about your being a reflective practitioner and about how you can help your TA engage in reflective practice. Reflective practice is now part of the accepted vocabulary of basic teacher training, with reflection on action (which is retrospective) and reflection in action (which occurs during the action, or teaching) widely accepted as being useful and conducive to raising standards in teaching and learning. However, we also made the distinction between reflection and critical reflection, where the former may largely be descriptive and the latter involves questioning the assumptions and meaning perspectives that underlie practice. We explored the merits of you and your TA collaborating on reflection, drawing again on constructivist assumptions that reflective discourse can enhance the potential for growth and learning – in this case, learning more about yourself as a teacher, as well as about the teaching situation and the pupils involved.

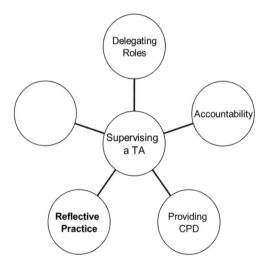

In Chapter 6 (Collaboration) we considered a variety of perspectives on collaboration – not only perspectives of who is involved in the collaborative process, but also perspectives on the purposes and formats of those collaborations. We see the need for collaboration as self-evident – that is, collaboration as a purposeful activity designed to promote and enhance learning opportunities, both for pupils, because of the collaboration between teachers and TAs, and for the teachers and TAs themselves as part of the learning community in the school/

classroom. Among the different perspectives, we referred to the work of authors and researchers such as:

◆   Sylvia McNamara and Gill Moreton who refer to collaboration as a means of increasing learning opportunities, as well as Jean Lave and Etienne Wenger who proposed a situated learning and apprenticeship model.
◆   Meredith Belbin who has researched teamwork extensively, and whose views offer useful insights for classroom teams.
◆   Peter Senge with his perspective from the field of business and management on the need for organizations to be deliberate in their attempts at being *learning* organizations.

Among these multiple perspectives, we hope that you found at least one that resonates with your own situation and offers insight into how you and your TA can work more effectively together.

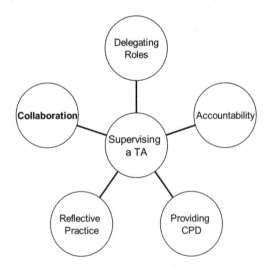

And lastly, in Chapter 7 (Logistics) we looked at some of the practicalities of supervision, including:

◆   time, because supervision does take time − time to prepare and plan (for and with your TA)
◆   evaluation, in terms of the less frequent performance appraisal type of evaluation that your TA may have (or that you may need to prompt if she does not already have such an evaluation)

◆ advocating for your TA, with the Head and other members of staff, in terms of your TA's status on the staff, supporting her requests for outside CPD (including necessary funding), and in terms of such things as letters of reference or other recommendations

◆ encouraging your TA to start developing a professional portfolio to document her growing skills and knowledge.

These are what we see as essential elements in supervising TAs:

◆ delegating roles and responsibilities
◆ monitoring and evaluating your TA's work
◆ providing development and growth opportunities for her
◆ engaging in – and encouraging her to engage in – reflective practice
◆ developing a true collaborative relationship
◆ working out the physical and logistical challenges of implementing all of the above.

These elements are based on our own experiences and those of teachers and TAs we have worked with over the years. The question often arises: Is there one that is pivotal or more important than the others? We think so. And that is a careful and detailed definition of your TA's role. If you did nothing else as a supervisor, this in itself would go a long way towards enhancing your TA's effectiveness. But notice that we say *careful*, because it is not enough to merely assign a detailed list of tasks; that list must consist of carefully selected tasks based on the needs of your pupils and the skills of your TA. This was really where the debate about the employment and deployment of TAs started many years ago: What were *non-teaching staff* (as they were often called then) really supposed to do? And who should decide? It was, and is, a natural starting point of the debate.

These elements could be represented as hierarchical, shown in the following diagram in the form of a pyramid.

◆ Establishing the precise nature of your TA's role and responsibilities is an essential first step, so that she knows what is expected of her in the classroom and in relation to your teaching and the pupils' learning, which she is employed to support.

◆ Accountability must have a context, and in this case that context is the set of responsibilities assigned to your TA; likewise it would be impossible to evaluate your TA's work in any meaningful way without reference to her assigned roles and the detail of those roles.

◆ Professional development naturally follows on from the assessment you make of how well your TA carries out her responsibilities.

◆ Reflective practice could be seen as a 'higher order' activity building from the preceding basics.

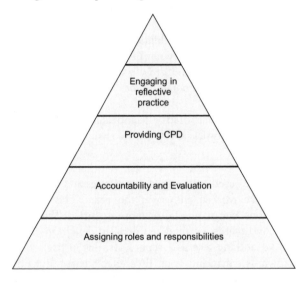

However, you could also argue that the elements of Accountability/ Evaluation and CPD are interchangeable on the diagram – or that they occur simultaneously, particularly if you accept a comprehensive definition of professional development. We would not necessarily disagree, but both must certainly be based on your TA's assigned responsibilities. You might also argue that reflection is an activity you can engage in from day one of working with your TA – that it is a vehicle rather than a step in the process. So then the elements would connect in a somewhat different way, as represented in the next figure.

Alternatively, you may see these elements as petals of a flower or cogs in a machine. However you view them, they are all most definitely interconnected and mutually beneficial. And, we would assert, all necessary for the effective supervision of a TA.

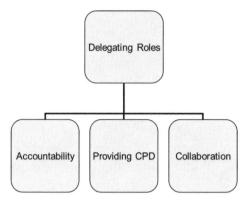

Where now?

So where do you go from here? In the Appendix you will find a variety of resources to help you in your supervisory role:

◆ background reading
◆ government documents and guidelines, and where you can access them
◆ references to the relevant literature, should you wish to investigate further
◆ resources specifically for TAs, including books and other publications, online materials and potential funding sources.

We would recommend that you make a plan of some sort in order to move forward in your supervisory role. On the basis of the SMART goals model, it would be advisable to ensure that what you aim for is Specific, Measurable, Attainable, Realistic and Timely. Select the area or element of supervision where you feel there is the most immediate need, and focus on one or two actions to begin with. For example:

◆ talking to my TA about the details of her job description so that we can each have an agreed written version for our files by the end of next week; *or*
◆ observing my TA (and taking notes) as she works with her maths group for 15 minutes next Thursday, paying particular attention to whether she gets all pupils to participate.

The role of a supervisor is not one to be taken lightly, and we applaud your evident wish to increase your understanding and skills in this area.

Appendix

In this appendix you will find a variety of different resources:

◆ details of books written specifically for TAs from several publishers
◆ websites for professional organizations that offer resources for TAs themselves or for teachers supervising TAs
◆ other websites of interest
◆ a list of references for the books and other professional publications we have referred to throughout the book.

Books written for TAs

Several publishers are now producing books specifically for TAs. Here is a selection.

Continuum (www.continuumbooks.com) has a *Teaching Assistant* series, which features books of general interest to TAs (for example, *The TA's Guide to Literacy* and *The TA's Guide to Behaviour Management*) as well as those addressing more specific additional learning needs (for example, *The TA's Guide to Dyslexia* and *The TA's Guide to ADHD*). On the Continuum website you can click on 'View series titles' and scroll down to the TA series. Other series that relate to education include: *Continuum One Hundreds*, *Special Educational Needs* and *Supporting Children* (this one is especially for TAs). In the general education catalogue you will also find *101 Essential Lists for Teaching Assistants.*

Paul Chapman (www.paulchapmanpublishing.co.uk). This publisher lists a number of books that would be useful for TAs – although they are not necessarily written specifically with TAs in mind. Two books you might be interested in are *Positive Approaches to Disruption in School* and *Resolving Behaviour Problems in Your School: A Practical Guide for Teachers and Support Staff.*

Sage Publications (www.sagepub.co.uk). A search on the Sage website using the term 'teaching assistant' will bring up a good list of books, including two that are specifically for TAs: *A Toolkit for the Effective Teaching Assistant* and *Supporting Children's Learning.*

Learning Matters (www.learningmatters.co.uk) has two series of particular interest to TAs: the Teaching Assistants' Handbooks, which includes *Supporting Learning in Primary Schools,* and the Higher Level Teaching Assistants series.

The publisher David Fulton has produced a number of books for TAs (including Glenys Fox's very popular and readable *Supporting Children with Behaviour Difficulties: A Guide for Assistants in Schools*). The David Fulton titles have now been absorbed into Routledge, although it may be easier to find information about them through www.amazon.co.uk rather than directly through Routledge.

A search on the www.amazon.co.uk website using the term 'teaching assistant' will also bring up a range of books written for TAs from a variety of other publishers.

There is also now a magazine specifically for TAs working in primary schools called *Learning Support.* It offers individual and school subscriptions, and each issue includes articles on a wide variety of topics relevant to TAs. Information can be found on the website, www.learningsupport.co.uk where there are also articles that can be downloaded for free.

Professional organizations

Several of the professional teaching organizations and unions now offer membership to TAs. Even without membership, it is usually possible to access basic information on their websites, and they often include information on government reports or legislation and policy. Here is a selection of teacher associations that offer particular benefits for TAs, together with their websites:

Association of Teachers and Lecturers (ATL) (www.atl.org.uk). ATL offers a free newsletter for TAs as well as training courses. Many of the courses are free to TAs who are members of ATL, and ATL will also sometimes offer travel costs for attending the training. In partnership with Higher Education, ATL also offers a pathway for obtaining credit towards a Foundation Degree, with up to 75 per cent of costs funded.

National Association for Special Educational Needs (NASEN) (www.nasen.org.uk). NASEN offers reduced membership subscription rates to TAs.

Voice (formerly known as the Professional Association of Teachers, which included the Professional Association of Nursery Nurses and Professionals Allied to Teaching) (www.voicetheunion.org.uk). Voice offers reduced membership costs for support staff.

Websites of interest

The Department for Children Schools and Families (DCSF, formerly the DfES) (www.dcsf.gov.uk)

This website offers information on a wide range of topics of interest, including the Early Years Foundation Stage. There are also research reports relating to TAs and their work, for example the 'Deployment and impact of support staff in schools', carried out by the University of London's Institute of Education. Enter the keywords 'national questionnaire' in the search box.

On the government's Standards site (www.standards.dfes.gov.uk) you can also find the materials we referred to in Chapter 1: 'The effective management of Teaching Assistants to improve standards in Literacy and Mathematics'.

Direct Learning Limited (www.classroom-assistant.net)

This website has a wealth of information for teaching assistants, particularly relating to dyslexia. Articles and material on the website can be printed out free of charge for personal/professional use, provided the web address is always included.

The Evidence for Policy and Practice Information and Co-ordinating Centre (EPPI-Centre) (http://eppi.ioe.ac.uk/cms)

The EPPI-Centre at the Institute of Education (University of London) has three research reports relating to TAs. They can be downloaded from the website, and found by entering the search term 'teaching assistant'.

Foundation Degree Forward (FDF) (www.fdf.ac.uk)

FDF is a national (England) organization that was established to support the development and validation of Foundation degrees. Funded by the Higher Education Funding Council for England, it provides information on Foundation Degree programmes across the country – in all fields, not just education. The FDF database can be searched by region, which would enable your TA to find the nearest programme geographically to where she works/lives, with contact details and other useful information. Some of the Foundation Degree programmes are specific to TAs, others have a more general education or early years focus. New programmes are regularly being added to the database.

Grounds for Learning (www.gflscotland.org.uk)

This is the website for the Scottish arm of the UK charity Learning Through Landscapes (www.ltl.org.uk). Schools in Scotland can draw on the expertise of staff at 'Grounds for Learning' in order to make the most of the outdoor spaces available to them; in other parts of the UK schools can go directly to Learning through Landscapes.

Reflective Learning–UK (www.reflectivepractices.co.uk)

Reflective Learning characterizes itself as 'a values driven, not for profit, social enterprise working to improve lives and livelihoods through reflective learning'. The organization produces a journal, *Reflective Practice*, which publishes papers on: different kinds of reflective practice and their purposes; reflection and the generation of knowledge in particular professions; the way reflection can be most meaningfully taught and learned; and the links between reflection and the quality of a workplace.

The Scottish Centre for Research in Education (SCRE) (www.scre.ac.uk)

As the name suggests, this website provides information on a variety of aspects of education in Scotland. Particularly appropriate to your role as a supervisor of TAs is the report of the evaluation of Scotland's Classroom Assistant Initiative.

Skills4schools (www.skills4schools.org.uk)

Supported by the Union Learning Fund, this website was launched in 2005 and provides guidance on training and development opportunities for support staff.

Teachernet (www.teachernet.gov.uk)

You may already be familiar with this website but may not be aware of the range of information and resources for support staff as well as teachers it provides. If you go to the website and click on 'Whole school issues' and then 'Support staff', you will find links to government documents and guidance relating to TAs. There are also case studies that give examples of good practice in using support staff in a variety of roles, as well as training modules that schools in England are asked to use to provide induction training to TAs. The full materials are available for download. You do not have to be employed by an English LEA to access them. The induction materials cover such topics as behaviour management, child protection, ICT, SEN, and inclusion. You will also find links to a range of teacher associations and unions.

Teachers TV (www.teachers.tv)

Teachers TV has a range of clips that would be useful for TAs, which could be used as part of their professional development.

Training and Development Agency for Schools (TDA) (www.tda.gov.uk)

This website includes 'The support staff framework' listing a wide variety of formal qualifications appropriate for TAs in a variety of roles, details of the NOS, the requirements for HLTA status and TA induction materials. The 'School leaders' pages of the TDA website include a range of resources for helping to develop the potential of support staff.

The HLTA standards can be accessed through the TDA website by following the links to 'Support staff' and 'HLTA'.

Also on the TDA website you can find the document 'Schools for the future: Designing school grounds', designed to help schools make best use of their outdoor space as a learning environment. Follow the link to 'Teaching and learning', then 'Early years foundation stage'.

Bibliography

Allred, D. M., Morgan, J. and Ashbaker, B. Y. (2000), 'Available but not accessed: Resources to enhance paraeducators' skills and knowledge', *Theories and Practices in Supervision and Curriculum*, 11, 68–73.

Ashbaker, B. Y. and Minney, B. (2007), *Planning Your Paraprofessional's Path: An Administrator's Legal Compliance and Training Guide*. Arlington, Virginia: LRP Publications.

Balshaw, M. H. (1999), *Help in the Classroom*. London: David Fulton Publishers.

Balshaw, M. and Farrell, P. (2002), *Teaching Assistants: Practical Strategies for Effective Classroom Support*. London: David Fulton.

Bamberger, J. and Schon, D. A. (1983), 'Learning as reflective conversation with materials: Notes from work in progress', *Art Education*, 36, 2, 68–73.

Belbin, R. M. (1993), *Team Roles at Work*. Boston, MA Butterworth-Heinemann.

Birch, A. (2007), 'Do the practices of reflection and critical reflection of para-professionals on a Foundation Degree programme impact personally on the students themselves, and professionally on their classroom practice?', Swansea Institute of Higher Education. Unpublished Masters dissertation.

Blanchard, K. (1997), *Gung Ho: Turn on the People in Any Organization*. New York: William Morrow.

Brown, J. S., Collins, A. and Guguid, P. (1989), 'Situated cognition and the culture of learning', *Educational Researcher*, 18, 32–42.

Clayden, E., Desforges, C., Mills, C. and Rawson, W. (1994), 'Authentic activity and learning', *British Journal of Educational Studies*, 42, 2, 163–173.

Coots, J. J. and Stout, K. (2007), *Critical Reflections about Students with Special Needs: Stories from the Classroom*. Boston, MA: Pearson.

Cottrell, S. (2003), *The Study Skills Handbook*. London: Palgrave Macmillan.

DfES (2004), *Excellence and Enjoyment: Learning and Teaching in the Primary Years*. London: HMSO.

Fox, G. (2003), *A Handbook for Learning Support Assistants: Teachers and Assistants Working Together*. London: David Fulton.

French, N. K. (2003), *Managing Paraeducators in Your School: How to Hire, Train and Supervise Non-certified Staff*. Thousand Oaks, California: Corwin.

Fuchs, L. S., Fuchs, D., Hamlett, C. L. and Allinder, R. M. (1991), 'Effects of expert system advice within curriculum-based measurement on teacher planning and pupil achievement in spelling', *School Psychology Review*, 20, 49–66.

Fuchs, L. S., Fuchs, D., Hamlett, C. L. and Ferguson, C. (1992), 'Effects of expert system consultation within curriculum-based measurement using a reading maze task', *Exceptional Children*, 58, 436–450.

Fuchs, L. S., Fuchs, D., Hamlett, C. L., Thompson, A., Roberts, P. H., Kubec, P. and Stecker, P. M. (1994), 'Technical features of a mathematics concepts and applications curriculum-based measurement system', *Diagnostique*, 19, 4, 23–49.

Ghaye, A. and Ghaye, K. (1998), *Teaching and Learning through Critical Reflective Practice*. London: David Fulton.

Ghaye, T. and Lillyman, S. (2008), *The Reflective Mentor*. London: Quay Books.

Hancock, R. and Collins, J. (2004), *Primary Teaching Assistants: Learners and Learning*. London: David Fulton.

Kincheloe, J. L. (2008), *Critical Pedagogy Primer* (second edition). New York: Peter Lang Publishing.

Lave, J. and Wenger, E. (1991), *Situated Learning: Legitimate Peripheral Participation*. Cambridge: Cambridge University Press.

McNamara, S. and Moreton, G. (1997), *Understanding Differentiation: A Teacher's Guide*. London: David Fulton.

Medwell, J. and Wray, D. (1998), *Teaching English in Primary Schools: Handbook of Lesson Plans, Knowledge and Teaching Methods*. London: Letts Educational.

Mezirow, J. (2000), *Learning as Transformation: Critical Perspectives on a Theory in Progress*. San Francisco: Jossey-Bass.

Morgan, J., Ashbaker, B. Y. and Allred, D. (2000), 'Providing training for paraeducators: What motivates them to attend?', *The Researcher*, 15, 1, 50–55.

Pickett, A. (1999), *Strengthening Teacher/Provider-Paraeducator Teams: Guidelines for Paraeducator Roles, Preparation and Supervision*. New York: National Resource Center for Paraprofessionals, City University of New York.

Pickett, A. L. and Gerlach, K. (2003), *Supervising Paraeducators in School Settings: A Team Approach*. Austin, Texas: Pro-Ed.

Reagan, T. G., Case, C. W. and Brubacher, J. W. (1999), *Becoming a Reflective Educator: How to Build a Culture of Inquiry in the Schools* (second edition). Thousand Oaks, California: Corwin.

Sage, R. and Wilkie, M. (2004), *Supporting Learning in Primary Schools* (second edition). Exeter: Learning Matters Ltd.

Schön, D. A. (1987), *Educating the Reflective Practitioner: Toward a New Design for Teaching and Learning in the Professions*. San Francisco: Jossey-Bass.

Senge, P. (2006), *The Fifth Discipline: The Art and Practice of the Learning Organisation*. London: Random House Business.

Sergiovanni, T. J. and Starratt, R. J. (1993), *Supervision: A redefinition*. New York: McGraw-Hill.

Sosik, J. J. and Godshalk, V. M. (2000), 'Leadership styles, mentoring functions received, and job-related stress: A conceptual model and preliminary study', *Journal of Organizational Behavior*, 21, 4, 365–390.

Vasa, S. and Steckelberg, A. L. (1997), 'What teachers need to know about using paraprofessionals: Higher education's role'. Paper presented at the Annual Conference of the National Council of States for Inservice Education. ERIC Document Number: ED293230.

Stecker, P. M. and Fuchs, L. S. (2000), 'Effecting superior achievement using curriculum-based measurement: The importance of individual progress monitoring', *Learning Disability Research and Practice*, 15, 128–134.

Vincett, K., Cremin, H. and Thomas, G. (2005), *Teachers and Assistants Working Together*. Buckingham: Open University Press.

Walker, A. J. (1996), 'Cooperative learning in the college classroom', *Family Relations*, 45, 3, 327–335.